Newark & Sherwood

— Landscapes and Legends —

Text by George Wilkinson

Paintings by Penny Veys

Cottage Publications

First published by Cottage Publications,
an imprint of Laurel Cottage Ltd.
Donaghadee, N. Ireland 2009.
Copyrights Reserved.
© Illustrations by Penny Veys 2009.
© Text by George Wilkinson 2009.
All rights reserved.
No part of this book may be reproduced or stored on any media
without the express written permission of the publishers.
Design & origination in Northern Ireland.
Printed & bound in China.
ISBN 978 1 900935 77 7

The Author

George Wilkinson moved to the cottage in which he still resides in late 1941. Largely because of the training he received in HM Forces, he became an engineer. As a civilian he lectured to Ministry of Defence trainees and later at several colleges in Nottinghamshire and at Trent Polytechnic.

Always having an interest in local industrial history, with early retirement he studied local history methodology at the University of Nottingham. As his knowledge and reputation grew, magazine articles followed, mostly historically based, often featuring more obscure facts.

He is now a town guide and Chairman of Newark Civic Trust, both occupations highlighting the need for well-presented informative heritage trails. So far, he has, with a Trust colleague, co-authored four; a fifth is in preparation with at least another three more planned. He is also an active member of *Friends of the Leicester Trader,* a rescued Trent barge, the aims of which are to keep alive the history of the River Trent through the development of a floating mobile museum. With the author on board, it will have to have a newsletter, won't it?

The Artist

Penny Veys has lived near Newark for over 30 years. She studied Architecture and enjoys drawing all sorts of buildings in their environment.

In conjunction with a printing firm she has made many notable paintings of schools and colleges as well as local subjects.

Penny has travelled widely, always observing and recording people and places. Her sketches and photographs form the basis for many compositions. A keen gardener, she is happy to take commissions for house and garden portraits.

AUTHOR'S ACKNOWLEDGEMENTS

In researching this dissertation, I have lost count of the number of local history publications of the villages of the district. To list them all would inevitably result in some omissions either through inadvertence or my ignorance of their existence. Armed with gleaned knowledge from these excellent works before visiting your village has made my task both easier and informative, rendering the writing a most enjoyable experience.

For the many painstaking hours spent by individuals and by both small and large groups in compiling these village histories and the information and enjoyment I have gained from them, I am deeply indebted to you all.

My grateful appreciation too goes to Tim Warner and the staff at Newark Local Studies Library for their willingness to allow access to the many publications in the collection and also to Glyn Hughes and the staff of Newark museum for their unstinting support. Thanks too are due to Carolyn Scott for her patience and guidance and to my wife Gillian for typing my unreadable scrawl.

For any errors or omissions, I accept full responsibility.

ARTIST'S ACKNOWLEDGEMENTS

I gratefully acknowledge the help of Rachel Harrison, Property Manager of the Workhouse, Upton Road, Southwell, and the British Horological Institute, Upton Hall, Upton near Newark.

Contents

Welcome to Newark

⁓

Newark-upon-Trent, to use its correct name, lies virtually on the eastern edge of the alluvial Trent Valley which, at this point, is some eight miles wide. The county and district boundary with Lincolnshire, appropriately defined by Shire Dyke, adds another four miles to the east. Close by the River Trent, the market town was built historically on higher ground close by a convenient crossing point of the river by the north-south route later to become the Great North Road. Travellers from the hinterland converged on this crossing and the small settlement where they could exchange their wares not only with each other, but also with people passing through. This convergence was considerably enhanced by the relatively easy navigation afforded by the river, compared with the difficulties of travel by road, enabling an east-west trade also. The provision of wharves followed.

Newark is the usual appellation hereabouts. When the town warrants a mention by the national media, it is usually defined as Newark in Nottinghamshire, which it undoubtedly is, although such a description provides little help in locating the place in the minds of, say, someone in Sidcup.

Newark is a market town, granted its first charter in 1549 although this only gave sanctions to a fair in May, when goods from the hinterland would be interspersed with various entertainments, some of which would be offensive to modern sensibilities such as bear-baiting and cock-fighting. A bear-baiting post can still be found in Newark Market Place; the collar attached to it only having been recently removed for safe-keeping.

The boundaries of this book align roughly with the administrative area of Newark and Sherwood District Council formed in 1974, rather than the hinterland upon which the development of the town depended, although some reference to the historical area will be unavoidable.

It was no accident that the Romans constructed the Fosseway so close to the river at this point – the ease with which supplies could be brought upstream for their army was an attraction. This road further enhanced the accessibility of Newark and its future was assured. Newark became an inland port.

So important did the river crossing become that the Bishop of Lincoln, Alexander the Magnificent decided to build a bridge here and a castle to defend it. Since with a bridge, attack from the northwest theoretically would be easier. The first castle, a motte and bailey, was of wood, sited more or less where the Tourist Information Centre (formerly the Gilstrap Free Library) is now, suggesting that it was always the intention to replace it with something more substantial nearer to the river. Early in the 12th century application was made to the King for permission to divert the King's Highway in order to make room for a stone castle, the ruins of which still command a view over the full width of the Vale of Trent, about 9 miles to westward at this point and views north and south for as many miles, including unobstructed views of the river and bridge. An unnoticed advance by whatever means

or from any direction by an attacking force would be virtually impossible.

Newark is situated at the crossroads of the Great North Road (which runs north to south and is the main route from London to Edinburgh), the Fosse from north-east to south-west and the River Trent. A prehistoric track, Sewstern Lane, is believed to have crossed the Trent close by, the tidal influence having ceased a couple of miles downstream.

The Fosse is often wrongly called Fosseway, since Fosse means the road or way built by the Romans to transport supplies and men to their various outposts, stretching as it does from Lincoln to Exeter, and running close to the river making interchange possible. Roman remains have been discovered just north of the town and at Farndon just to the south, also very close to the river.

These three thoroughfares were to be the mainstay routes for many years. Most goods, from Roman times until the Turnpike Act, were transported by packhorses. The term packhorse is usually found in the singular and as such is misleading. It was more normal for safety from bandits and other advantages that they travelled in convoy. An example of a packhorse bridge is still to be found on the outskirts of Cotham, crossing to East Stoke parish and thence to the Trent. It has been opined recently that the bridge is far too narrow to permit such a use. The possibility that this is a replacement could surely be allowed.

The goods predominantly thus transported [wool] were brought to Newark and other Trent-side wharves to be loaded onto boats, which would transport them downstream to the Humber ports and thence to the continent. Evidence of this former prosperity still appears in a few places demonstrating the wide distribution of the trade such as in the naming of some Newark inns. The Pack Horse in the town centre was replaced in the suburbs by an inn of the same name in 1852 when the population expanded out of the town and the Woolpack, originally built as a rich wool merchant's house, subsequently opened as a public house, its name reflecting its past.

An improved system of transport was to be established – the age of the Turnpike. By this means towns, villages and cities were obliged to provide and maintain roads and surfaces that would permit coach travel even in inclement weather; previously the roads were rendered well-nigh impassable in wintertime. Coach travel was to make Newark prosperous yet again. Horses needed to be changed every twelve miles or so, less still in hilly terrain. Coaches on the Great North Road would change at Grantham on the way northward, again at Newark,

and yet again at Retford. At least three inns in the town had facilities for 90 horses; most provided horses for hire too and a blacksmith. This, in addition to the victualling, provided a substantial income to the innkeepers.

Newark had three tollhouses all still in existence – though not for the collection of tolls – until 2007 when one was demolished. One, on Beacon Hill, stands restored but derelict, the other by Trent Bridge partly but sensitively rebuilt and now the headquarters of the Nottinghamshire branch of the Women's Institute.

Tolls were levied on the number of wheels for coaches, drays and wagons and on pigs, cows, horses, geese and presumably any other livestock. Drovers, or drifters, herded cattle and sheep long distances, taking them from this locality to cities where they would then be fattened up for Christmas. Toll bars were avoided if at all possible by this fraternity although such practice was illegal, and cross-country routes that they used were called drove ways or drift ways. A road between Coddington and Winthorpe is actually called Drove Lane and there are other examples. It is commonplace to find country lanes that have forty feet between hedges yet the metalled road is only fourteen feet. These are frequently old drift ways. Only one third of the road was in use at any one time, the route chosen being the one in best condition. A few examples here are between Hockerton and Southwell, Upton and Caunton, South Scarle and Collingham. There are countless others.

The Sleaford to Farnsfield Road, passing through Newark was also turnpiked, thus adding another spoke to the transport wheel. The section of the Fosse from Lincoln to Newark was never turnpiked, but on the south-west side of the town it was. At the end of Thorpe Lane in East Stoke stands the one-time toll house, in deference to its subsequent role as the residence of the keeper of the nearby wharf. Just a few yards further on, the coach route left the Fosse to join with Church Lane, East Stoke before making its way to Hazelford Ferry and thence through Bleasby en route for Nottingham.

Then came the railways, first the Midland in 1846 which joined Nottingham and Lincoln, passing through Newark roughly half-way. Most line-side villages had a station, thus at a stroke enabling these villages easier access to towns. Six years later followed the Great Northern Railway joining London and Edinburgh and affording line-side villages similar opportunities. That both railways came to Newark was a most fortunate coincidence. This circumstance completed the transport hub that was to enhance the town's economy, albeit at the expense of the coaching industry which, in places like Ollerton with no railway, was a disaster.

The medieval wedge-shaped, cobbled marketplace, a listed monument in its own right, contributed to the continuous importance of trading to Newark. Until the middle of the 20th century, Newark market was thriving. Almost regardless of the weather, but often complaining about the cobbles, housewives thronged into the market, the number swelled on a Wednesday by farmers' wives who had come to town with their husbands, the men to trade in the cattle market, the ladies to purchase supplies for the week. The attraction of this busy market was much appreciated too by shopkeepers, particularly those that lined the sides of the market place, but all enjoyed substantial increase in trade on market days.

On Saturdays, wives were frequently accompanied by husbands, often reluctant companions, together with their children, home from school, protesting vociferously. Children and shopping do not usually go together well. All this changed in 1974 when the markets were no longer administered by the Town Council, but by the newly formed District Council.

Farm animals of all descriptions came to a separate market, still called Beast Market Hill to this day although the attractions now are the impressive Ossington Coffee Tavern on one hand and on the other the Gilstrap Centre, once the public library, now home to the Tourist Information Centre, the Castle Story, and the Castle itself now a listed monument which, although ruinous is still very impressive, still guarding the bridge.

At the south-east corner of the market square is a wonderful timber-framed building, The Olde White Hart, parts of which were built in 1313. Facing the square, it has a most ornate front and imposing carriage entrance. Locals will tell you that the pierced fretwork ornamentation bears a striking resemblance to the altar screen in the parish church, dedicated to St. Mary Magdalene. So far, so good. The story continues that the woodcarvers and carpenters took a long time to complete the altar screen and, being unable to pay their bills, were tasked by the landlord to provide ornament for the front of the inn. True or not, it is a credit to the craftsmen who executed the work. The colours too are reckoned to be authentic.

Eight miles away Southwell also has a beautiful timber-framed building, the Saracen's Head at the top of Church Street. It was here that King Charles I spent his last night as a free man, although a much troubled one, before riding to Newark to order garrison to lay down their arms and march out proudly as undefeated before surrendering himself into captivity of the Scots at Kelham on May 8th 1646. King Charles was eventually beheaded in 1649. Perhaps it is significant that the Saracen's Head was known as the King's

Head at that time.

There are magnificent 18th century wall paintings in the Bramley Room at the Saracen's Head just as there are wall paintings too in several of the timber-framed houses of Newark, but none to equal the splendour of the former.

In Southwell too, there is a high proportion of Georgian houses suggesting a similar drastic replacement of earlier buildings. This trend has continued in more recent times, houses of this type being demolished to make way for the new market place. Buildings in the old market place in Westgate were demolished at the same time to reveal the gable end of another timber house. Mainline railways missed Southwell and as a result, the town never became industrialised so logically there are few remains. A branch line of the Midland Railway from Rolleston to Southwell was never a real success. Administration in this town has always centred on church activities. It is partly the importance of the Minster that is directly responsible for the continued expansion of the town. Attracted to Southwell by this magnificent cathedral are countless tourists, a boon to the trade of the place.

The Minster with its twin pepper-pot towers and exquisite Norman architecture, masonry and carving is a most imposing building. Reckoned to be unique in that there are nine renditions of green man here more than any other church in England. Tombs and memorials of numerous worthies abound, as they do in the no less imposing St. Mary Magdalene in Newark, which, with its slender pillars and high ceiling in the nave, presents a much more elegant appearance than the much more substantial Romanesque pillars of Southwell.

Hops were grown around Southwell and names such as Hopyard Farm are fairly commonly found. These hops were very bitter and with the advent of the railway age, breweries opted for the less astringent Kentish hops. It is probable too, that each producer traditionally grew a favourite variety of hop plant. Brewers opted for consistency. Cultivation of hops was widespread too in Ollerton, there being no less than six flourishing businesses in 1830, some hops finding their way to nearby Rufford Abbey although normally they had a surplus, which they sold.

Equally, many villages had malthouses, in early days on estate farms and manor house enclaves where it was common practice for women to undertake both malting and brewing. Only when the trade became commercialised did it become an almost exclusively male preserve. One or two malt kilns dotted about the area serve as reminders of the time when ale was the safest form of drink, the brews of those days safe to drink and more nourishing too than the much weaker modern equivalent. In those days most estates had a small brewhouse, where ale for the estate workers was brewed. Small beer – beer that is brewed afterwards when the first brew, the stronger beer, destined for the top table had been taken – was much weaker than the first brew, so much so that it was considered suitable for children, hence the appellation 'small beer'.

At the top of King Street in Southwell stands Burgage Manor. Poet Byron, who later became the sixth Lord Byron, stayed at Burgage Manor for eight years with his mother around 1800. He hated his stay there, writing two volumes of poetry, one of which, *Hours of Idleness,* he wrote to while away the hours of boredom. Later it was also to be the home of Richard Warwick, director of a burgeoning brewery in Newark.

Standing on the approaches to Southwell is the most complete and best-preserved Workhouse in Britain, a reminder of harsher times past. A marvellous piece of Georgian architecture it stands defiant on high ground and must have been a very daunting prospect to the poor wretches who had little choice but to approach its doors. Not as daunting however as the scene inside. Even to modern visitors who gain comfort from their early escape, there is the smell and claustrophobic closeness of the walls of the long, dimly lit passages and long, bare, gloomy stairs.

Numerous minor rivers network their way across the Newark and Sherwood District. The river Greet, having powered the mill at Maythorne only a short distance upstream from Southwell, to paraphrase Tennyson; rushes beneath Caudwell's mill in Southwell, *'winds about all in and out'* to Upton mill then *'bickers down the valley'* to Rolleston, *'to join the brimming river'* Trent. Between them they must almost equal the output of Newark's three watermills and five windmills, particularly since it is unlikely that all five windmills were functioning at the same time. An informant, tongue in cheek perhaps, conjectured that some were taken down because there was insufficient wind for five. If the post mill at Upton, of which only the base remains, the watermill at Fiskerton and the watermill at Kelham on the Trent are taken into account, there can be no doubt that the success of the area depended on this bread-basket. Many of these are still serving as monuments to a bygone era, some ruinous and some converted to houses but the tower mill at Tuxford has been restored and now again mills commercially when the wind conditions permit.

Not far away hidden in a wood is one of Britain's saviours in the Second World War – Eakring oil field. Eakring is a small village with a big past. Duke's Wood hides much of what was a very active oil field producing high quality, low sulphur oil, ideal for aviation fuel. A few Nodding Donkeys are still working, although most are now removed, a relevant heritage centre houses a fine collection of oil-field memorabilia and there is a monument to the 'rednecks', the American oil engineers who toiled to drill the wells. The woods themselves are now a wildlife park for a range of birds not to mention being host to bee orchids – the waste from the wells providing the ideal soil conditions.

Close by Laxton still maintains the old strip system, boundaries being allocated and disputed at the annual court leet, held of course in the local pub where customary shilling fires are now paid in larger amounts. With a well-appointed heritage centre and a pinfold opposite, the pub has moved from its original site elsewhere in the village.

As the rich account of Newark and the surrounding district unfolds in the following pages, a clearer picture of the history will emerge, from a snapshot of brewing in the area to the workhouses and mills – a small embroidered sampler of the tapestry which makes up the Newark story.

In 1870, when this structure was erected as an oil-crushing mill by James Clark, the River Trent was still an important highway for heavy, bulky goods, even though by this date Newark boasted two railways. The river provided convenient transport upstream to Nottingham and beyond, and downstream to Hull and thence to the continent. In this instance fuel for the boiler furnaces came from the Nottinghamshire coalfields, whilst the raw materials for the oil and cake mill were cole seeds (rape) and linseed.

Oil is extracted by crushing the oil-bearing seeds in a cylinder press, the resultant empty seeds being pressed into cakes which were broken up and used for cattle feed, the oil for lamps and linseed oil for preserving and smoothing wood shafts for hand tools. Willow, widely grown in the Trent valley, was not all destined for the basket-making industry widespread in the area, but some for the cricket bat industry of Nottingham. Linseed oil was used for them too.

In its heyday up to 200 barges were to be found overnight in the Basin, as the stretch of water at the foot of the walls is called. Traffic now is predominantly pleasure craft.

At the downstream end of the building, still bearing the sign *The*

Swans on the Trent

Trent Navigation Company, is another tall building at right angles to the first. Originally a malthouse, it was bought by the Trent Navigation Company when it became redundant, a fifth floor added and converted in 1880 to a warehouse for river borne goods. Downstairs lies The Navigation, an authentic themed pub whilst upstairs has been converted to offices.

The flat-decked bridge was, until 1952, a hump-backed brick construction with a typical semi-circular arch. This was inadequate for the 82 foot petrol tankers that plied the river at that time, bound for Nottingham. The bridge provided access to the water driven corn mill until that burned down in 1965.

It was by this bridge that in the severe winter of 1895 that ice-skating was practiced and even an ox was spit roasted on the ice. Such cold weather was dreaded by the river folk. Their poorly paid existence was insufficient to allow for the enforced idleness of being frozen in. Whilst the conditions were enjoyed by some, many more faced great hardship. A thaw would have been a very welcome Christmas present.

The Trent Navigation

NEWARK

In its heyday the complex of buildings on this site were most impressive, a culmination of the gradual but inexorable development of the renowned malting and brewing industries in Newark. The ventilation cowls atop the kilns were designed so that whatever the direction of the wind, the flower design vane ensured that the cowl always turned its back to it, thus creating suction to draw the moist air from the kiln.

Built in 1854 this malting was the first development on this site to be followed 17 years later with the first of the brewery buildings with new extensions appearing periodically, the last nearly 50 years after the first. Despite the purely practical purpose, this Victorian business fraternity ensured that their premises were also works of art. No expense was spared in either the design, or execution, a far cry from the image of 'Satanic mills' with their soot blackened austerity. Different coloured bricks were used to highlight features and colonnaded façades disguised the purely practical loading bays. A small oriel window breaks up the flat face of the brickwork but had several practical uses. North light was very much favoured in those times and, in malting and brewing, was essential when examining barley samples of grain as it casts no shadows. Standing forward of the building line, the window also afforded management the advantage of overt observation of activities in the yard below.

When built, the brewery was not obscured by buildings or bridges on this side, but would be visible to all who approached Newark along the Fosse from Lincoln. Travellers on the Great Northern Railway, constructed a score or so years earlier, would have had a full view; a wonderful advertisement.

The south elevation is equally impressive. Here the oriel windows are of similar design, although much larger, this being the side where senior management worked. With the advent of the railway came an increasing development line-side. Malthouses began to obscure the brewery vista in the late 1890s followed by a bridge over the railway in 1935, until then served by a level crossing. In order not to lose the advantage of advertisement an office block was constructed right up to the pavement of Northgate. The boardroom here had a huge oriel window permitting views of the full length of the road. Surmounting this window is a magnificent terracotta coat of arms, not unlike that of Newark. Conversion of the whole complex to luxury apartments on upper storeys and elegant boutiques below will ensure the future of this wonderful epitaph to the malting and brewing industry of the town.

The Brewery, Northgate

NEWARK

The Maltings at the brewery, Newark

Built in the 14th century as an extension to the 12th century castle, the curtain wall would have presented an awe-inspiring spectacle. With its freshly worked Ancaster limestone gleaming a honeyed white in the sunshine, it would almost shout *power*. Even today, minus the crenellations atop the walls adding another five feet or so and having weathered to a light grey, pock-marked by Parliamentary canon balls in the English Civil War and natural degradation of five and a half centuries, it is still impressive.

The square tower remains are part of the 12th century castle, but the two more northerly multi-angular towers are part of this new build. Each tower has its own dungeon, those beneath the tower closest to the bridge being the most remarkable. One, a bottle dungeon on account of the roof resembling the shape of a wine bottle, was known as an *oubliette* – Norman French for 'forgotten', as most of the souls incarcerated therein were. The other, a barrel-roofed dungeon, was reputedly used as a slaughterhouse in more recent times and at some stage, as living accommodation. It is a myth that these dungeons are below ground, although having descended a steep ladder to gain entry, visitors may be excused for thinking so. Viewed from outside, the floor level corresponds with the top of the plinth, some twelve feet above river level.

Apart from the main entrance, described elsewhere, the water gate was the only other access to

Civil War Soldiers

and from the castle. Almost all supplies were brought in this way via a stone staircase to the undercroft, it being the storehouse for food, arms and hardware. At the opposite end it still has a flight of stone stairs, which would originally have given access to the main banqueting hall. The arrow-loop windows can also be seen twenty feet or so up the wall.

What is now a pleasant shrub-lined walkway immediately in front of the square tower, and leading to the town centre, is still to this day called Cuckstool Wharf. It enabled access to the river for the cuckstool or ducking stool, a popular punishment for scolding women and for merchants who gave short measure. Although its use was feasible punishment for both sexes, women were mostly those so punished. The last use in Newark was in 1810 and appears to have been the final use of such devices in Britain.

Newark Castle

Curtain Wall

NEWARK

18

Nestled in the corner of the Market Place in Queen's Head Court lies a small, detached, timber-framed building, known presently as The Tea Shoppe. The Queen's Head Inn that gave its name to the court is now renamed Hobgoblin, itself also a timber-framed establishment, which hides the Tea Shoppe from those who frequent the market, affording it a quiet seclusion.

In the early 1960s the then Department of the Environment launched the system of listed buildings, bringing to a halt the 'knock it down and redevelop' phase prevalent in the post WWII years. In 1961 restoration of both the Queen's Head and the Tea Shoppe were undertaken.

Formerly a baker's shop belonging to W. Ash, there were adjoining buildings, one of which was the bakery. With the exception of the shop, the other buildings were so decayed that they were demolished and new build took their place. The Tea Shoppe was deemed worthy of conservation, although during the execution it was decided that the building should be disassembled and rebuilt to the original design and using as much of the materials as possible, at the same time ensuring that it complied with modern building regulations. Shortly afterwards it emerged as a Prudential Assurance office. Its present use as a café is more fitting!

On the wall are reproductions of photographs of the yard as it was in living memory. One picture shows the same baker's float and horse used by Mr Ash throughout WWII to deliver bread, needing no petrol of course. A similar system was used by the local dairy. This system has advantages even over the electric floats now employed. Spoken commands to the horse obviated any need for the driver to remount the vehicle as he navigated from house to house.

Newspaper reports at the time announced with surprise that the rendered visage of the Queen's Head concealed the timber framing seen today. Both buildings display timbers within although those in the teashop, especially upstairs, have been made into more of a feature, fascinating to contemplate whilst savouring a cafetière of real coffee and a homemade scone. Authenticity both without and within has been maintained as far as practicable, the most significant change being the windows in the gable end, a wall that originally abutted the house next door and which needed no windows.

The Tea Shoppe,
Queen's Head Court

NEWARK

Newark is fortunate in still having a significant number of timber-framed houses, a number of which, with the classical black timbers and white plaster, are self-evident. Even more are intact but are now hidden by brickwork added in the Georgian era. The tallest and most impressive has to be the Governor's House in Stodman Street.

At three storeys and broadside to the street, each level has coved jettying, a feature which allows each successive level to encroach an extra two feet into the street. Originally built for a rich merchant in the English Civil War, it obviously had the status and space to be suitable for the Town Governor to have as his headquarters, affording him the convenience of the Parish Church across the square, where look-outs were posted in the gallery atop the tower, and close enough to the castle to permit easy communication with the soldiery there. Perhaps, being out of the main line of fire of the Parliamentary army cannons, he was able to enjoy some hospitality at the local inns, although the town being under siege, supplies of victuals were very limited.

There is an account that a Parliamentary spy had so accurately described the premises that the besieging Parliamentary forces deliberately targeted it with their cannon. It is stated that the intended target, the Governor's house, was only saved by the fact that just across the street, on the site of what is now the NatWest bank, was a house very similar in style to the Governor's House which confused the gunners and it hence became the target.

Here it was that one Hercules Clay lived with his wife and numerous children. During one siege he dreamt that his house had caught fire and was so alarmed by it that he roused the household, servants and all, and directed that they should leave the premises. Nothing happened and everyone went back to bed. Hercules was again awakened by his dream, and once again evacuated to the market place. On this occasion, a blazing bomb landed on the premises, setting fire to it. These incendiary devices were very effective, most roofs being thatched.

So grateful for his deliverance was Mr Clay that he left a sum of money sufficient to provide for a church service every March 11th. Although the money has been spent, being no match for inflation, the traditional service is still held, with one of his relatives attending.

The Governor's House

NEWARK

On approaching Newark by highway, byway or railway, the elegant spire of the Church of St. Mary Magdalene can be seen standing guard over the town as it nestles in the bottom of the Trent Valley, just as it has done for over 900 years, silently guiding travellers like some speechless, unerring sat nav. Closer to in the adjacent streets or from the cobbled market place, the full majesty of the edifice can be appreciated.

Nothing remains of the Saxon church, but progressively larger contributions from the next four main periods of development are clearly evident. From the Norman phase just four piers and the crypt still exist; the square tower together with an octagonal spire, which soars to over 250 feet, was added in mid-13th century and possibly an extension to the chancel too. A south aisle in the decorated style was added during the first half of the 14th century as too was the plinth for a north aisle, but completion was curtailed by the well-documented outbreak of Black Death. This enhancement was completed in the Perpendicular style between 1390 and 1500 and finally in 1520 the addition of north and south porches and vestry.

It is believed that prior to 1770 the church clock was not sited on the tower but possibly on the main fabric of the church. A new clock was fitted 9 years later and served well over 100 years although in its latter years had become unreliable. A new clock was completed on St. Mary Magdalene's Day (22nd July) 1898. Curiously this clock has faces on north, east and west of 7 feet diameter but that facing the Market Place, the south face, is 9 feet in diameter.

It is a privilege to venture inside to marvel at the lofty splendour of the architecture, illuminated on sunny days by light shining through the magnificent stained glass windows; monuments to the great and the good of yesteryear. The muffled chimes of the clock above serve as a reminder of the passage of time surrounded by a centuries old feeling of timelessness.

Parish Church of
St. Mary Magdelene

NEWARK

In 1140 the Bishop Alexander of Lincoln asked permission of King Henry I to divert the King's Highway to facilitate the building of a castle and a bridge nearby. The very existence of ruins testifies that permission was forthcoming.

Stone-built atop the river terrace, thereby adding about 10 feet to the height and, gleaming white, it would have been an awe-inspiring prospect to travellers, hostile or otherwise. The valley here is wide, low-lying and at that time covered with nothing more than scrub – surprise attacks would have been virtually impossible.

The two multi-angular towers and curtain wall that still face the river today were added in the 14th century. However, substantial parts of the earlier structure still survive. Square towers and semi-circular arches are typical characteristics of the Romanesque period; the towers and grand entrance, reputedly the best-preserved Romanesque keep in Britain, are wonderful examples. Provided with neither portcullis nor drawbridge, it is probable that a form of timber bridge across the wide moat had some sort of barrier. Timber bridges can be set alight as a last resort of defence by those within, or of course by the attackers should they manage to get close enough, either way leaving no alternative to the attackers but to cross a wide smelly moat while suffering a barrage of all manner of projectiles, not to mention various noxious liquids, hurled by the besieged within.

Four dungeons are still accessible and one of them, a prime example of bottle dungeon [called an oubliette, meaning forgotten] bears testament to the treatment of prisoners. As food was reserved for staff and more welcome visitors, those incarcerated below had a curtailed life expectancy.

Whilst standing in the intact 14th century undercroft, a group of teenagers, having learned the strategy of arrow loops and use of the water gate, were invited as they left to observe the half exposed Saxon skeleton at the turn of the stairs. "What! A real live skeleton!" exclaimed one female member of the party, who then left at great speed!

Newark Castle

NEWARK

Stretching for almost half the length of Boar Lane, the bookshop is really a terrace of three cottages, disguised in early Georgian times by an outer shell of brickwork and dormers fitted with Yorkshire sliding sash windows. Inspection within reveals the substantial oak woodwork of timber-framed buildings. One beam therein has been tree ring dated to around 1588. Later in the Georgian era the complex was converted to shops.

From Middlegate it is possible to see the truncated gable end of another more substantial property. To the right of the newer Georgian three storey house can be seen the truncated gable of the other end, the centre section of the timber-framed house being demolished to make way for it.

This street-facing gable end now offers into a coffee shop, converted recently from buildings used as storage by the provender millers and, more recently within living memory, suppliers of pet foods too. Within the coffee shop, a Victorian fireplace is still in situ and upstairs are three similar Victorian fireplaces, confirming that these too were originally three cottages, again timber-framed.

As in so many businesses in the market town of Newark, redolence of the agricultural influence can be observed. The earliest records are sufficiently precise as to location to indicate that the owner was a flour miller and seedsman; the seeds here presumably rye, wheat, barley and root crops. Only supplies of flour came from local windmills. Strays owned the windmill just up river at Farndon, although by this time flour was being milled by new processes, augmenting the variable reliability of wind power by the provision of steam power which rendered windmills and water mills redundant.

Later, new ways of milling flour were developed at the importing docks and supplanted the locally produced flour with a cheaper product. Many mills changed to provender milling producing food for livestock. This one was no exception. The tower of Farndon Mill still stands, without sails and capped and is used now just for storage.

No longer with any agricultural connections, other than a few books on the subject, the book store has reincarnated this interesting complex of buildings, which was beginning to show its age.

Stray's Bookshop

NEWARK

The Town Trades Guilds, who used to meet in Moot Hall on the north side of the Market Place, fearing competition and loss of monopoly, engaged in protectionist activities and refused to allow new trades to set up in Newark. On one occasion a linen draper applied to trade in the town, but permission was denied because the Guildsmen could not see what possible benefit to the town such a trade might be and furthermore might encourage application from such nefarious trades as maltsters and brewers to set up business.

Frustrated by such blatant protectionism, the Mayor and Aldermen agreed to sell land to erect a multi-purpose building on the main market square on 26th January 1773. Mr John Carr drew up plans, the necessary Act was obtained and an advertisement in December 1773 was placed in both *The York Courant* and *The Nottingham Advertiser* to the effect that a Plan and Elevations of the intended new Town Hall could be viewed at Mr Brough's office in Newark and that of Mr John Carr in York in order to attract the necessary tradesmen to build it.

Mostly, it was Newark tradesmen that answered the call, although Christopher Theakston of Doncaster carved the statue of justice that stands atop the centre pediment to one side of which is a unicorn and on the other a lion.

Building began in 1774. On the ground floor the area at the top of the front steps was used as a corn market, although frequently altogether more congenial surroundings were sought in the back room of the Ram Inn in Castle Gate. Beyond this area is a colonnaded hall intended for the sale of butter. An open area beyond this was designated as shambles, later to become a market hall built in 1908. The whole ground floor complex is known today as The Buttermarket.

Upstairs can be found the ballroom with its magnificent decorated Adam style ceiling, while to the front the Council Chamber, 35 ft long and 16 ft high, offers onto the loggia affording wonderful views of the market square mostly surrounded as it is by fine Georgian buildings, once the houses of successful businessmen, now converted to more lowly shops and apartments.

The Town Hall

NEWARK

An 1806 picture of Ridges shop and the Market Place appeared in the *English Illustrated Magazine,* February 1897. Except for the addition of a late Victorian shop window and door facing the Market Place, the appearance of this iconic building looks very much as it did when visited by the young Lord Byron. Only the name over the door has changed. At that time it was the premises of Samuel & John Ridge, printers and booksellers.

Whilst the young Byron was living with his mother at Burgage Manor in Southwell, he composed two works of poetry, *Fugitive Pieces* and *Hours of Idleness,* both works the outcome of the boredom he suffered whilst living there. Having written the poems, the urge to have them printed afforded him an ideal excuse to travel to Newark, a distance of some eight miles, which in modern sensibilities is nothing more than a small inconvenience, but much more significant using horses.

It was at the Saracen's Head Inn just a couple of score paces across the Market Place that Byron lodged for the few days it took to print his works. Doubtless, although what passed for his entertainment is not recorded, he made full use of the time in more exciting pursuits than could be enjoyed at home in Southwell.

Burgage Manor

The Saracen's Head Inn in Newark now houses Barclay's Bank. The entrance to the printer's shop, with its classical oval fanlight, portico and two steps remains completely unaltered. Byron skipped up these 2 steps as best he could with his lame foot and gave with the brass knocker his hurried rap-a-tap which, from its peculiarity, always foretold his awaiting presence without. Behind this door is the very same staircase, now offering to a coffee bar on the first floor.

The printing press used by the Ridge brothers was, until the recent retirement of printer Roy Stephenson, still in use by him, first at his various business premises and latterly at Newark Millgate Folk Museum, where Roy used to give demonstrations. All of the type and the press itself can still be viewed at the Millgate museum.

Byron's Printers Shop

NEWARK

A couple of years after John Smeaton had built his 125 arches in order to raise the Great North Road above the flood plain, the Duke of Newcastle had plans drawn up for a new bridge across the Trent to replace the old flat timber-decked one, whose stone piles were too close together to allow square-rigged barges to pass through. Built in brick with stone facing, it was completed in 1775 with seven arches. In order to recoup the expenses a tollhouse was built on the right hand side. It is still there, having had several lives since then. Presently it is the headquarters of Nottinghamshire Women's Institute, having been the warehouse and office of an agricultural merchant between times.

Opposite, Lady Ossington built the Ossington Coffee Palace in 1883, in essence a Temperance Hotel, on the site of the old cattle market still known as Beast Market Hill. The Palace was in memory of her husband, Lord Dennison, who was speaker in the House of Commons and had recently died. A condition laid down in Lady Ossington's will was that alcohol was never to be sold there and that any transgression would be cursed. The embargo was eventually lifted, but several businesses selling alcohol did not prosper.

Truly an architectural masterpiece, the pargetted panels which are all different and are on all sides, are echoed on the top storey by carved wood panels. There are plaster images of The Green Man along with other plaques all depicting ecclesiastical themes.

The popularity of the newly opened Midland Railway in 1846 rendered the bridge no longer adequate for purpose. To address the need of the extra pedestrians, the bridge was widened a couple of years later by the addition of pavements on either side, cantilevered by means of cast iron beams laid cross ways with decking between. Cast iron railings were added at this time with no less than four cast iron coats of arms at the crown, each painted in full colour, the pair facing the road also bearing the town motto *Deo fretus erumpe,* as well as the date 1848 in Roman numerals. Use of ornamental cast iron to achieve a practical purpose was a fitting and enduring advertisement of the skills and prosperity of local foundries at that time. Examples of ornamental cast iron abound in the town, as do more fundamental examples such as coalhole covers, ventilators and support pillars although both of the latter are rapidly disappearing as modern development takes its toll.

The Trent Bridge

NEWARK

This building was originally two houses, both timber-framed; the left hand one from the 16th century, the other from the 17th. Within living memory, the ground floor was home to three businesses. The left one used to be a greengrocer's whilst the right was used as a fishmonger's and up the passage alongside, the small lean-to seen to the right of the vignette still carries the sign *'W. Bush, licensed to sell game and poultry'*, just as it has been for a century, though crazed and faded now.

From the street the impression of a continuous roof is deceptive. When built, both would have been thatched, but when the changeover to pan-tiles was made, it would prove easier and quicker and therefore cheaper, to conceal the different levels under one roof.

At the rear, it can be seen that the older house extends for some considerable distance up St. Leonard's Court. This was the building that gave its name to the yard. Although it was established protocol for all royal ladies to be chaperoned by a retinue of attendants rather than in the modern sense, an occasion arose during the Civil War when Queen Henrietta Maria had need of safe lodgings and, being unchaperoned, it was felt fitting and appropriate that a safe ha-

St. Leonard's Court

ven would be with the monks who ran St. Leonard's Hospital, of which the house formed part.

Upstairs, now a bijou café called King Charles Coffee House, there are exquisite medieval wall paintings. Below, all three units are now combined as a florist's shop, its wares tumbling out onto the pavement, just as they would have in Victorian times.

Watson Fothergill designed the building next door. He was an architect with a passion for incorporating design features from a selection of historic eras, and here we have stained glass, Georgian porticos, barley sugar twist balusters, garden gate finials, terracotta features and polychromic brick. They are all here.

Selected by the Newark and Nottingham Bank to design new branches, Fothergill's ambitions were curtailed somewhat in Newark by the size of the site. Given a freer reign in Nottingham, many other architectural elements are incorporated.

King Charles

Coffee House

NEWARK

36

Built on land originally given to Archbishop Oscutel of York by King Edwy in 956, the first recorded occupant of a hall was Robert Bagenham in 1335.

In 1620 one Owen Oglethorpe lived here, and at the time of the Civil War Martin Oglethorpe, probably his son, was squire. Part of the Elizabethan Hall can still be found, incorporated in the main structure of the present building. Designed in 1828 by W. H. Donthorne for Thomas Wright. A member of the Nottingham family of bankers, Donthorne later became a founder member of Royal Institute British Architects.

As part of the celebrations for Queen Victoria's coronation in 1838, a procession marched through the village, ending at Upton Hall where everyone enjoyed a feast of roast beef and plum pudding followed by a dance. At this time, there were ten servants 'living in', and others in the village. The Wright family remained as owners until 1857 when it was purchased by Mr Philip Faulkner, a Newark solicitor, County Coroner for 30 years and Mayor of Newark in 1833. Mr Faulkner had six servants living in and others in the village. A daughter, Harriett, married Lucas Brodhurst, a member of the prosperous family of maltsters of Mansfield but owning malthouses in Newark too.

Sold in 1895 to John Francis Warwick, a director of Warwick and Richardson, brewers and maltsters of Newark, who remodelled the interior and added the west wing incorporating a ballroom with a stage, a games room and a further six bedrooms.

Many village functions were held there.

In 1939, at the onset of war, the Fathers of the Holy Ghost bought the property from Sir Albert Ball, but as it was requisitioned to house evacuees, the Fathers only took up residence in 1945, using it as a Roman Catholic Theological College.

It has been home to the British Horological Institute since 1972 with a dedicated reference library and a museum as well as a large collection of antique longcase clocks. Also of local interest, the museum holds the original works of Newark Northgate Station clock which was rescued from a skip and donated to the Institute after it was removed in 2002 for safety reasons, having been installed originally in 1853.

Upton Hall

UPTON

Built with oolitic limestone from Ancaster, a high quality stone that being so evenly grained is perfect for intricate masonry, and durable too, Hawton Church has abundant features that admirably demonstrate the skills of the craftsmen who carved and built it.

It is reasoned by local historian Rev. Quarrell, long time incumbent of the parish, that this stone was probably transported from Ancaster in Lincolnshire by means of the River Witham, the Car Dyke and the River Devon, by which stands the Church of All Saints.

All Saints by any standard is a very large church for such a small parish. Upon the south side are several scratch dials, also known as mass dials, which seems a more appropriate name. They were an early and primitive form of sundial whereby a shallow hole is drilled into the stonework into which a stick could be inserted casting a shadow upon the dial, which was marked to coincide with the times of the masses to be celebrated within. That there are several such dials suggests quite a number of persons were present in pre-Reformation days. The exquisitely carved Easter Sepulchre is claimed to be the best in the country.

The River Devon, pronounced 'dee von' hereabouts, comprises three rivers; the River Whipple becomes the River Smite before finally becoming the River Devon, a tributary of the Trent which joins that most important waterway just upstream of Newark, usefully augmenting the flow. Puzzled visitors to the district frequently ask why the word Devon is pronounced differently from the county of Devon. Perhaps it would be more fitting to enquire of Devonians why they are different.

At the left hand side of the Devon mouth is Newark Rowing Club and on the opposite bank a large boat yard supplying and maintaining the river cruisers which now predominate as river traffic, freight now being almost totally a part of Newark's history.

Hawton Church and River Devon

HAWTON

Standing isolated in the middle of a field in Sibthorpe is a Grade I listed building, one of only 22 listed in the whole of Nottinghamshire, but is the largest in the county. Built around 1340 the dovecote provides, around its honeycombed walls, 1148 nesting places. Each aperture is 4½ inches square and offers to a nesting space behind it some 18 inches deep, within the 36 inch thick stone walls. The condition of the structure is perfect and judging by the accumulated guano inside, still finds modern avian tenants. Curiously, the door is only 3' 6" high, a ploy, apparently, to prevent theft of birds in large hampers. What prevented thefts by use of several smaller hampers, is not conjectured.

At 45 feet high, it stands amid numerous ancient fishponds, dry now and grassed, but once stocked with fish, such provision being a mark of status and wealth. Standing beside the Carr Dyke, which provided fresh water, it was the ideal spot for the construction of the 13th century church tower and the addition of a chancel around 1340 by Thomas de Sibthorpe. At this date, the structure was enlarged to form a religious college. Remember, the collective noun is a college of bishops. Occupants of the college at this time comprised 8 chaplains, 3 clerks, a warden, a sacristan and additional lay staff, probably about 20 persons in all.

The keeping of pigeons as a year

The Dovecote, Sibthorpe

round source of eggs and meat is traditionally attributed to the Romans, although this is pure speculation. It is difficult to believe that ancient Brits had not already developed a partiality for pigeon pie. A more reasonable conjecture would be that the Romans adapted and refined the culture and means of accommodation when they arrived. The keeping of pigeons on such a scale declined when farming practices improved, allowing cows, pigs and sheep to be available year round.

However nothing lasts forever and by the end of the 14th century the college had entered a period of decline which culminated in its closure in 1540. By 1790 nothing remained except the dovecote. Signs of previous roof lines and corbels on the outer wall on the north side, which supported earlier roof arches of additional buildings remind visitors of the earlier complex, when all features would have been inside. Huge 19th century chest tombs testify to the wealth of some of the families in the village, but the ages of some of the inhumed – 23 and 25 year olds for instance, demonstrate that wealth cannot buy health!

The Dovecote and Church of St. Peter

SIBTHORPE

The Bromley Arms was bought and extended by Lord Bromley so that, it is said, he could hunt on both sides of the river. The pub sign, just visible, has the coat of arms of Samuel Smith, the banker (later Lord Bromley) with the motto *Pense forte*. The motto is a play on words. Pauncefote is a family name, Samuel being a brother in law of Lilian Pauncefote, a daughter of Julian Pauncefote, the first ambassador to the newly formed America. Smith was owner and resident in the 19th century of Stoke Hall where he was Lord of the Manor.

Standing on the East Stoke bank by the ruins of the ferryman's slipway looking towards the wharf opposite, observing the visitors to the Bromley Arms enjoying the sunshine and a meal or pint as they sit chatting around tables, gives an impression of a continuum of leisurely lifestyle. This is not dispelled by the presence of river craft – luxury cabin cruisers and lesser versions, some moored alongside the quay, others gently making their way upstream whilst a slightly anomalous narrow boat cruiser goes with the flow towards Newark.

Opposite the Bromley Arms, at the other side of the quay, stands what was quite obviously a malthouse and kilns, the latter converted into a house, the former to a boathouse serving the needs of today's boaters. Its rather utilitarian appearance serves as a reminder of the hustle and bustle of a busy wharf and ferry terminus. Barley from the countryside around was ofttimes transported by river as was barley imported from abroad, the river giving easy access to Hull and other Humber ports.

Malt was produced here by James Hole of Caunton, having continued in the trade of his father Samuel who had several maltings at Carlton-on-Trent. The Holes grew barley on their own lands near, and in, Muskham but increasingly, demands for malt from Nottingham breweries and others necessitated additional supplies of barley. Not only was importation of barley needed in years of bad harvest, but facilitated the export of malt.

A hundred yards or so downstream was a very much larger wharf and buildings, although now just used as a car park for sightseers, and a perch for fishermen. Fiskerton flourmill stands across the road, straddling the River Greet, the final commercial use of this river before it discharges here into the Trent.

The Bromley Arms

FISKERTON

Whereas windmills are totally dependent upon wind of a sufficient speed to turn the sails, but not so fierce and fast as to break them, watermills were sited where a fast-flowing stream or river was available to provide motive power. Sufficient head of water could be guaranteed by construction of a millpond, with a leet to allow any excess to bypass the mill.

Rolleston Mill is just one of several sited on the River Greet. Disused now, it stands rather forlorn although the adjoining mill keeper's cottage is occupied. The mill race, having passed beneath the mill, is most attractive, the ripples catching the morning light before the stream reaches the simple railway bridge carrying the Nottingham-Lincoln line. Built in 1846, the route is now plied by diesel engined trains which replaced the much more attractive steam trains of yesteryear. Meanwhile the River Greet relentlessly makes a journey of half a mile or so, where it was called upon until recently to power Fiskerton Mill before discharging into the River Trent a short distance away.

Rolleston Mill stands at the north-east corner of Southwell Racecourse, the Greet forming one boundary of the course, and allows access to the front of the mill where the carefully constructed bridge, weirs and leet remind visitors of the skill of the millwrights and associated tradesmen who harnessed the raw power of the river; further reminders of the agrarian dependency of the district.

The death knell of most village mills was sounded by the invention of the huge steam-powered roller mills sited at the docks, producing the refined products so commonplace today. Many millers, no longer having a demand for flour, concentrated on milling meal for stock feed, but most now are disused, except where the process can be used as a part of an educational curriculum, or as a visitor attraction producing organic products with teashop. Sadly this is not the case here.

Rolleston Mill

ROLLESTON

Step in my friends, and take a cup
It is not dark, for the moon is up
Sit down, refresh, and pay your way
Then you will call another day.

Those simple words outside The Full Moon pub in Morton no longer portray the full nature of a village inn once a retreat for village workers, eager to lubricate their tired bones after a day's hard graft. Fine food and entertainment are the modern norm.

Events at Morton include 'A Festival of Morris' on Plough Sunday although the title does it little justice. Morris dancers from all over the district assemble and perform in the wide street before the pub. They are joined by mummers and clog dancers, each group ensuring a continuous entertainment for an ever-changing group of visitors. Many schools in the area congregate to compete in the Junior Morris competition, each group tutored and accompanied by a teacher, passionately and competently performing their variation of this ancient pastime.

Refreshments for their labours and for the gathered crowd is provided in the specially erected marquee, where fare includes beef burgers and hot dogs and a refreshing drink. For those who fancy something more adult, the inside of the inn beckons.

Scarecrows adorn street corners and other village spots as part of another traditional celebration. This competition is judged, of course, by The Full Moon.

These traditional entertainments reflect the farming influence of the area. Take a fascinating walk along any of the numerous streets to discover the more serious reminders of an agricultural dependency. The pinfold for example, wherein stray cattle or sheep could be impounded, until a fine payable to the pinder was duly paid. Restored in 1987 for the Parish Council by the Newark Community Project, although ivy-mantled now and, in spring, carpeted by shimmering yellow celandines, it could be doubtless pressed into service should the need arise, but seldom, if ever, does.

The Full Moon Pub

MORTON

Quite obviously a timber-framed building since its restoration in the 1960s when the rather plain render was removed, the Saracen's Head has had a chequered history. Foremost in the minds of many is the story of King Charles I spending his last night of freedom here, before surrendering himself to the Scottish contingent of the Parliamentary army and being taken to Kelham. This was May 5th 1646. Dating by dendrochronology yields a date of 1450-1463 from 3 roof samples taken so the inn was already more than 200 years old by then. A framed facsimile copy of the death warrant is displayed in the reception area.

It is fairly apparent that travellers on the road from Newark to Mansfield using any means of transport could enter through the archway from Church Street and into the Saracen's Head yard, tarry a while and then continue in the same direction to exit directly onto the Farnsfield Road, or of course, vice versa.

Over the years, the premises have been extended to incorporate the inn next door. The range of outbuildings on the north side of the yard, once a hive of activities from ostlers' quarters, carriage sheds, stables and probably a blacksmith's shop are now largely unused. An ambitious plan to use this redundant range to house a Southwell Heritage Centre has now

Saracen's Head

been shelved. Many people, whether locals or not, are unaware of some rather splendid 16th century wall paintings in the room over the arch. In the front parlour is a fine display of old crockery. Until recently a superstition regarding one of the plates, which was upside down, was that should anyone turn the plate right way up, the business was doomed to failure. A recent visitor observed that the plate has been rotated to its correct orientation but with no apparent effect on the viability of the business.

The Saracen's Head is one of the ports of call on whistle stop tours covering Britain in a week. For some unexplained reason there is a great enthusiasm for photographs to be taken in the yard together with the notice displayed, which reveals that the Rotary Club meets there. The other 'must see' item on the itinerary is the Minster. As much as half an hour is allowed to visit this brace of historical establishments.

Truly these monuments warrant much more time than that.

Saracen's Head

SOUTHWELL

Sunday Telegraph, October 11th 1998

Workhouses marked an important milestone in social history and the one in Southwell was built in 1824 by Rev. John Becher, a local philanthropist, and George Nicholls, who later became a Poor Law Commissioner.

A magnificent example of Georgian architecture, portraying an air of menace with its clinically exact proportions sitting on the hillside, the arched window hoods raised like supercilious eyebrows and yet at the same moment looking like downcast mouths. Curtainless, the blind windows beneath them were like cold eyes gazing down on the desperate wretches slowly making their way up the slope to an uncertain reception, passing as they did so the luckier inmates toiling in the gardens to provide part of the meagre rations doled out within.

Other tasks also performed by those classified as the idle poor were breaking rocks for road mending, breaking bones for fertiliser or picking oakum – old hemp rope used for caulking the hulls of ships. Frugality and austerity went hand in hand to deter all but the most desperate from making application to enter. The description of workhouse conditions by Charles Dickens in *Oliver Twist* paints a detailed picture of what life was really like in city workhouses. In establishments like Southwell, treatment was less severe and rations a little more generous.

Even today, entering those echoing passageways, decorated only with lime-wash, to reach stone stairs, disappearing at the top, one flight for men and another for women and yet another for children, has a most foreboding air. The windows appear like prison bars and the sight outside of trees and grass and sunshine a tantalising dream. Visitors can take comfort in the certain knowledge that in half an hour they will be able to resample that dream. No such luxury was forthcoming for the inmates, forced to submit themselves to this life of hardship.

The Workhouse

SOUTHWELL

Approach the town of Southwell from the east on the Hockerton Road early on a sunny morning in spring time and see Southwell Minster bathed in golden light. Reflecting this royal illumination the stones glow with an inviting honey hue. From this vantage point the whole of the cathedral can be viewed, the town looking deceptively small. As the road descends into the valley, the Minster disappears for a short period, to reappear suddenly alongside in the town centre. The two pepper-pot towers at the west end, a feature unique in England, can be seen from here. Between them stands the huge west window with the grand west doorway beneath.

It is difficult to find fault with this mother church of Nottinghamshire, but the refenestrated west window has given rise to controversy. With its delicate colours, resplendent in the setting sun, it is felt by some to lack substance. For them, the pale shades do not reflect the splendour that surrounds them. On the other hand, the strident colours of the more ancient windows are held to be too brash and loud, although the afternoon sun shining through them projects a kaleidoscope of muted colours on the otherwise plain drum pillars of the nave.

On reflection, it is these very same broad Norman pillars, simple in style and ornamentation, that impart a message of great strength, solidity and powerful in purpose; properties which symbolically represent the whole purpose of the Church.

Green Man
Southwell Minster

In contrast, the very much more ornate and slender columns of the Gothic Chapter House entrance entice the visitor to enter to see the exquisitely executed, intricate carving of the pillar capitals, the Leaves of Southwell, for which the Minster is, justifiably, widely renowned. There are equally impressive carvings within the octagonal chapter house itself.

Ornamentation, seemingly impossible to equal, adorn both sides of the chancel screen, the east side being even grander than the west side. Looking out of the quire, the plain pillars of the nave serve as a peaceful backdrop to the spectacle.

The north exterior, readily viewed from the street, allows everyone to observe and appreciate the hundreds of symmetrical carved chevrons that surround every feature. It is impossible to estimate how many stonemasons there were employed, nor how long they were about this task. From the uniformity of the pattern it can be conjectured that they used templates in the execution of their tedious task, especially when compared with the intricate and different carving of their successors.

Southwell Minster

SOUTHWELL

Mention Sherwood Forest to anyone nationally and it immediately conjures up images of the Major Oak, the wicked Sheriff of Nottingham and Robin Hood, apart from a few dissenters from other counties who lay claim to the latter. Hands off! Romantic connections aside, there is much more to Sherwood Forest than that.

Newark, Southwell and Ollerton each have examples of timber-framed houses or inns, as do many of the villages in the area. Mostly, though not exclusively, these used local oak for the main structure before filling the interstices with wattle and daub and as a preservative giving the walls, timber and all a lime-wash finish – painting the timbers black was a Victorian fad, not a historical feature.

Sherwood provided much of the timber for these buildings and, until an edict from the King forbade the use of oak other than for military purposes (ships mainly), this tradition continued,

although some economies were already in effect because supplies of suitably sized timber had already been commandeered. An example of the necessary economy in timber use can be seen in the construction of the King Charles Coffee House compared with the earlier Olde White Hart building.

That oak is a durable wood is admira-

The Olde White Hart, Newark

bly evidenced by the continued existence of these timber-framed dwellings and inns, the earliest being the rear ranges of The Olde White Hart in Newark dating from 1313, a date obtained by the relatively new technique of dendrochronology. Were it not for the widespread use of Sherwood oaks in this area, obtaining a reliable database would have been much more complicated.

The Major Oak, symbolic of Nottinghamshire for centuries, stands isolated now within a ring fence to protect the surrounding soil from further compaction by the feet of the thousands of visitors. Several of the branches are supported now by steel poles, a zimmer-frame for a venerable lady of the forest. Clones of the tree have been taken and grow elsewhere in the forest to ensure that the subject of legend continues for centuries to come.

Sherwood Oaks

EDWINSTOWE

When spring arrives in Rufford there can be no doubt. Bluebells carpet the considerable area of woodland, so much so that the ground almost disappears in a blue sea of stems with their bell-shaped flowers swaying gently in the breeze.

The numerous trees towering over them, providing the dappled sunshine needed by this British native wild flower, are mostly Norwegian maple related to the more commonly found sycamore, but different in several respects. Deep green leaves and beautifully contrasting lime green racemes of flowers appear together, unlike the sycamore with its clustered lime green flowers appearing on an otherwise naked tree. All maples are renowned for their autumn splendour giving them the distinction not only of heralding the spring but also bringing autumn to a close.

Part of the original Cistercian Abbey in Rufford can still be seen, although substantial demolition of much of this complex was necessarily carried out in 1956, years of neglect having taken their toll. There is still much to see however. The now roofless monks' dormitory, the vaulted dining hall of the lay brothers, part of the Cloister Walk and other features may still be visited.

Long before the invention of refrigeration, preserving food – other than by salting or pickling for instance, was problematic. Winters were much harder then and ice several inches thick would form on the lakes and streams and the means to harvest this bounty and store it were devised.

There were five ice houses at Rufford, of which only three remain. Essentially an icehouse is a deep hole in the ground, lined with brick or stone situated under trees to shield it from the sun. Into this pit are placed chunks of ice, broken from the covering of the Black Lake, the largest lake at Rufford and which supplied water to the Abbey. Each layer was covered with straw partly as an insulator and partly to prevent successive layers from freezing together thus making an impenetrable mass. The top of the ice heap was then covered with a thick layer of straw, and likewise the doorway. In this manner, ice could be kept, sometimes for a couple of years. Although it was customary for the doors to face north, at Rufford they face the lake for convenience. In later years ice from high lakes in Norway was imported, supplies being more reliable and the quality much higher. The last use of the ice houses was in 1936.

Bluebell Wood

RUFFORD

The family tree of the brothers John and Robert Mettam can be traced back to 1635. Throughout that time Mettams have been millers in the area; the earliest records have them at Kneesall windmill. A few generations later records locate them at Eakring, also at a windmill.

The grandfather of the two present owners worked Eakring mill until the end of World War II; their father, who came to Ollerton watermill around 1900, was a coal merchant during the day, rising at six o'clock to be sure of first place in the queue at the pit to pick up supplies. In the evening he would then grind wheat for flour until bedtime. This regime continued until about 1950 when steel roller mills at the docks made milling flour unviable. Work here continued however, grinding corn for animal feed, probably barley, for the next eighteen years.

1862 saw the replacement of the fourteen foot diameter mill wheel, about eight feet across, the paddles originally of wood, but now steel scoops. Now in some need of repair, it is planned to replace the backboards in 2009.

Although fully functional, commercial milling here has ceased. Periodically demonstrations can be seen both to ensure the functionality of the works and as a means of enlightenment about our heritage.

There are three sets of stones. Two sets are of Derbyshire stone and one set of French burr. Derbyshire stone is coarser texture and used mainly for animal feed. The finer French burr would be used to grind flour. Over a period of time, as milling continues, the stones wear thinner, rendering the grooves in the grinding surfaces too thin. On these occasions Father Mettam would remove the 3 ½ hundred weight stone, by hand and alone, turn it, and redress the stone by chasing out the grooves to a suitable depth using a tool designed for the purpose.

From time to time someone offering his services as a stone dresser would call. To check the truth of his claims he would be challenged with the words: "Show us yer metal!" Bona fide dressers would have hands pitted with stone chips whereas less reputable workers would not.

The Water Mill

OLLERTON

Built in the reign if Charles I, the first hall at Thoresby was remodelled in 1685-7 but burned down in 1745 with few things rescued. A new hall, designed by John Carr of York was built shortly afterwards. This was torn down by Earl Manvers and the present hall, designed by Anthony Salvin was erected between 1865 and 1875. The grand south front, dating to c.1900, was built further away from the Spanish Chestnut Grove and the little stream which he considered too close to be healthy. It boasted steamboats on the lake and a fine herd of deer. With a circumference of ten miles, Thoresby Park covered perhaps 2000 acres of forest mainly oak, beech and Spanish Chestnut.

The magnificent hammer beam roof of The Great Hall truly is a sight to behold, as too is the famous carved chimney piece in the library featuring the figures of Robin Hood, Little John and the Major Oak. When built there was room enough for 50 guests and their servants. It is most unlikely that the Hall was ever occupied to full capacity until the recent acquisition by Warner Hotels and its renovation and conversion to a luxury hotel and spa.

During the many prolonged absences of the Manvers family, access was granted to the Hall in order that the splendour of both the exterior and the interior, with its many beautiful objects and furniture, could be enjoyed by lesser mortals. Access to experience the grandeur may still be had, of course, by becoming a paying guest. Thoresby Hall is one of the finest stately homes and, sitting secluded in 2000 acres of Sherwood parkland, it still enjoys the best setting of all stately homes as it did even when most were in their prime.

An avenue of beech trees lined the original carriage entrance, an impressive spectacle known locally as 'Thoresby Cathedral'. Imagine emerging from this avenue to confront the enormous hall by a lake. These trees were, alas, felled in 1949 and used for tool handles.

Thoresby Hall

THORESBY

Most people will remember from school days the basic principal of the Open Field System. Sometimes only two fields were involved and sometimes four, but three was the most common, as it was, and is, in Laxton. It has been so for seven centuries.

The *Domesday Book* of 1086 records six plough teams at Laxton. This equates to about 720 acres under cultivation. Also there were extensive woodlands and common land, which would have provided grazing, fuel and other necessities. It seems probable that at this period there were two fields, but by the early medieval period the three field system was well established.

Each field was divided into strips which were allocated so as to ensure that everyone had pieces of good, bad and indifferent qualities. The strips in those times were fairly narrow and are considerably wider nowadays in order to permit the use of modern farm machinery.

It was, and is, essential that crops be grown on a three-year rotation, such as winter-sown wheat, spring sown barley or peas and the third year fallow, the grass and weeds providing grazing. The number of animals has declined over time and in 1967 rules were changed to allow the growing of forage crops on the fallow.

What is now a unique system is not the only distinction of Laxton, for it has the best-preserved motte and bailey castle in Nottinghamshire dating, probably, from the late 11th century. With a height of 71 ft and a diameter of 816 ft, built on a hill 220 ft high, it would have commanded a clear view over much of this area of Nottinghamshire. Even today the view is stunning, though the patchwork of the smaller fields of modern farming give a totally different outlook from that experienced nine centuries ago.

By the Dovecote Inn is a well-equipped interpretation centre. Inside, those wanting to learn more can study a faithfully reproduced map of the strips or watch an explanatory video. The rules governing the procedures and transgressions were administered by a council which met in the Dovecote Inn. It still does, although fines are now a little more than a shilling.

The Pinfold, Laxton

Laxton

THE DOVECOTE AT LAXTON

No further evidence is needed to confirm that the site of Tuxford Mill near the top of the hill is ideal; the siting of three windmills virtually on the same spot near the top of Tuxford Hill shows that. At 34 ft high, the tower mill is not a giant; obviously greater height was unnecessary, serving to corroborate the notion of an ideal placement.

Built around 1820 with four storeys, it was tarred black, a common enough means at that time of affording protection from wet weather. The sails turned anti-clockwise, not a widely adopted trait.

Milling continued here until Thursday 21st April 1885 when the mill, owned by Mr Firth of Ranskill, was extensively damaged by lightning. *The Miller* magazine reported that the gas meter was hurled through a window, taking the frame with it. The miller, Mr Longbottom, had the whiskers and skin on one side of his face burnt. Use of gas or steam power was a widespread custom amongst millers; an insurance against periods of little or no wind ensuring that work could continue independently of wind conditions. Wind of course continued to be used as a free and renewable source of energy when available. There was no resumption of milling after the explosion.

In 1982 the derelict mill was bought by the Ostick family who, aided by Fred Savage, a retired woodwork teacher, began restoration. After much hard work and solving many problems, the repairs were fully completed in May 1993, when it became the third working mill in Nottinghamshire.

The Osticks opened the mill on occasion to give demonstrations to parties of visitors and on Heritage Open Days but never actually worked the mill commercially. This was left to Paul Wyman and his wife Fari, who bought the mill and still run it today. Paul, who had some experience of milling, undertakes the actual milling using only wind power, using periods of little wind to bag up the different varieties of flour. Paul can also be found regularly at local farmers' markets, from where he sells the products of his labours, at the same time promoting the mill's facilities.

Alongside are a busy tea and coffee shop and a retail flour counter, which is run by Fari.

Tuxford Windmill

TUXFORD

Holme Church of St. Giles dates from the mid 15th century, although first impressions are that it is probably much older. Built by John Barton, a rich wool merchant of the day, the south aisle, parvise and porch are testament to his piety and wealth. He also built a substantial stone house nearby. The chimney breast displayed the Barton coat of arms whilst in the stables was the couplet,

'I thank God, and ever shall,
It is the shepe hath payed for all.'

The house, alas, no longer stands.

It is unusual to find a room over the porch in a village church, such things more normally being found in the churches of towns. Known as Nan Scott's Chamber in support of the legend that one Nan Scott withdrew to the confines of this room when Holme was infested with the plague and of such an affliction she was supposedly the only survivor. Quite how she got food is not clear. Perhaps she caught rabbits, the churchyard being home to a number of them.

Over the porch entrance are seven shields of arms, mostly belonging to John Barton and his family although two bear the arms of the Staples of Calais. These latter arms and merchants' marks also appear on both the tower and both sides of the west window. They also occur on the buttresses of North Muskham church on the opposite bank.

Holme and North Muskham were, until the mid-16th century, one and the same settlement with the River Trent flowing about a mile to the east. However, presumably after a serious flood, the river chose the more westward route that it now follows even though the old channel is still very much in evidence near Langford church and Manor House where, except in flood times, it is now a grassy hollow.

In Holme village is the stump of an old cross with an almost complete counterpart in Muskham. These monuments, sited at either end of the route of the ferry, were used by ferry passengers to commit themselves to God before venturing the perils of the waters.

Holme Church

HOLME

Approaching Kelham Hall on the road from Newark, glimpses of the building can be occasionally caught from a distance, but turning the final corner reveals the hall in all its 19th century Gothic style glory.

Architect George Gilbert Scott had been engaged by owner Mr Manners-Sutton to repair and modify the building designed by John Sanderson c. 1730, but whilst these changes were being executed, fire in 1857 gutted most of the original building. This gave Scott the opportunity to incorporate 'every invention and improvement', many of which were probably witnessed at the Great Exhibition of 1851. Foundations were laid in April 1859 and the building was virtually completed by June of 1861.

Some people including scholar of architecture Pevsner are paradoxically critical of the mixture of window styles and lack of symmetry, but equally complain of lack of variety in the brickwork. George Gilbert Scott came to Kelham having spent the years 1852 to 1855 on extensive restoration of Newark Parish Church and having already designed the Houses of Parliament and many other distinguished projects. That he later went on to design St. Pancras Station is testament to the notion that such criticism was not shared by Scott's contemporaries.

Signs of over-budget problems, which

Kelham Hall

oft besets many modern building schemes, can be witnessed inside. For whatever reason the full design was never completed. Columns in many rooms and corridors have no marble shafts although plinth and capitals indicate the intentions and intricate carving on doors completed in some examples, in course of execution in others with completed motifs at the top, basic carving in the middle and unstarted at the bottom, all indications of cessation of work. The planned conservatory was never built either. Nevertheless, it is a fascinating example of 19th century architecture both within and without.

Seen here backlit by the evening sun, Kelham Hall has an air of magical mystery but in winter, when the leafless trees permit a less obscured view, silhouetted against a grey sky and reflected in the waters of the in spate Trent, it assumes an air of brooding dominance. In autumn lit by a full moon with swirling mist rising from the river in front and drifting into the trees, it is reminiscent of early scenes in a Hammer horror film.

Kelham Hall

NEWARK

From the window of the preserved tower of Upton post-mill the whole vista of that part of the Trent Vale in which Newark lies can be seen. Framed on the left by Mickleborough Hill which, in days of yore, helped channel the wind to the mill, which stands on a ridge of lesser elevation close-by. Together they define the western edge of the valley. Framing the far right is the rapidly growing new Staythorpe Power Station.

Viewed in springtime or autumn whilst the early morning mist is gradually burned off, each element of the panorama is randomly revealed as the haze clears, seconds later to be obscured again and another landmark becomes momentarily bathed in sunshine. An hour later, all is revealed and the magical awakening of the sleepy town is over.

Debdale Hill, three miles or so north of Upton Mill and some ten metres higher provides another vantage point. Looking down into the valley bottom as so many travellers, farmers and workers have done over the ages, the town of Newark is seen, surrounded on all sides by green countryside, demonstrating in an instance the description of a small agricultural market town, nestling by the River Trent. The spire of the Parish Church once again punctuates the scene. Bathed in sunshine the whole scene is one of enchantment.

A fall of snow miraculously changes the whole vista to resemble the picture on a Christmas card. Undulations, unnoticed before,

now become emphasised, hedges accentuated by snow drifted against them. Looking down on Newark, the darkness of the houses contrast sharply with the snow, the intriguing multi-level roof line of the streets silhouetted against a leaden sky.

How easy it is to imagine oneself riding in a stagecoach, large flakes of snow transforming the scenery as twilight accentuates the welcoming lights of the town below, the steaming horses seeming to quicken their pace, knowing that food and rest are close, the passengers eager too for the welcoming fire and cheery landlord at a traditional inn.

Alas, the dream is shattered! These days the cosy inns are banks and building societies, and the stables boutiques.

A Panorama

NEWARK

A Brief Miscellany

THE GEORGIAN PERIOD

Visitors to Newark frequently remark that the town is lucky not to have lost much of its Georgian heritage to the 'Knock it All Down and Rebuild Brigade'. Certainly evidence abounds to illustrate a Georgian influence. There is a super-abundance of Georgian-style houses here; even though many are actually Victorian, they still carry many of the classical hallmarks of the earlier era.

In 1725 the Duke of Newcastle declared that Castlegate was too narrow to accommodate the increasing traffic flow and should be widened. Without much further ado the width of the road was increased, regardless of consequences for anyone who lived there; or was it? It is easy to believe that there was a continuous row of houses more or less the whole length as it is now, but this is unlikely. Frequently, descriptions in leases and deeds will speak of *'messuage with appurtenances together with stable and garden'*. The stable implies enough space

for access. Furthermore, the number of leases for Castlegate is not huge, but nevertheless some displacement of people must have occurred. Mostly these were better quality houses, owned by the up and coming newly rich industrialists and businessmen.

Reference to Attenburrow's map of 1790 still shows a gap between the Boar Lane range and that of Castle Gate. At around 65 years, the rebuild programme was an extended one. The map also shows that the widening of Castlegate and most of the construction of what amounts to terraces of large, imposing houses was complete except for a few at the south end. It was boom time for all connected with the building trade.

The foregoing discussion concentrates on the Great North Road but redevelopment was widespread throughout the town. In the Market Place a similar scenario was unfolding in the demolition of existing properties to facilitate the construction of the Town Hall. Throughout the town there is evidence of similar activity. Rev. Bernard Wilson had a whole street built in 1772. This boom time for developers was to continue apace with the grand schemes of the Georgians giving way to the expansion due to the embryonic Industrial Age. Even the much-decried hovels of the yards needed labour and bricks and the services of the ancillary trades. A few remains of privies survive, but gone are the 'thunder boxes' with pit or bucket. New uses, mostly storage, have been found for these appurtenances.

The 1770s was a turbulent but expansive period nationwide, Newark included. Eighteenth century roads were being improved as a result of Turnpike Acts. Newark was greatly affected in that the Great North Road from Newark Castle to Muskham Bridge crossed the particularly low-lying flood plain, rendering it muddy and often impassable in winter and in times of flood. John Smeaton, an engineer who also designed the second Eddystone lighthouse, was commissioned to build a viaduct following this route to elevate the road across the flood plain. This he did by constructing several series of arches each set across a channel of the braided river comprising 105 arches in all, 86 of which still exist, many of them still performing their designated purpose.

This viaduct was built in 1772; quite an engineering tri-umph. The actual design of each individual arch reveals a tenuous confirmation of the use of agricultural labourers. The distance between the centres of the piers is 16ft 6ins and the arches are 33ft wide, dimensions which would have been familiar to agricultural workers because a common measuring tool in farming at the time was the rod which is of course 16ft 6ins long.

In view of the speed of erection the number of people involved must have been high; not only labourers, but brick-makers, brick-layers, carters, lime-burners, carpenters, saw-yers to name but a few. There was an accelerated exodus of agricultural labourers from the countryside to the towns seeking employment, a consequence of enclosure of the open fields of the villages with the subsequent conversion to pasture requiring less labour. Finding employment for these people was, apart from the accrued benefit of a much-improved road, an excellent strategy. A considerable sudden demand for poor relief would be averted.

A group of businessmen formed the Trent Navigation Company, which commissioned William Jessop to devise a scheme to ensure a minimum depth of 2 feet of water in the Trent at all times. Jessop, who had been apprenticed to John Smeaton with a colleague, surveyed the Trent from Cavendish Bridge (now Shardlow) to Gainsborough, marking all the deeps and shallows. The Trent Navigation Commissioners eventually settled for a minimum depth of 2' 6", the standard depth for canals. This project also required much labour. Considerable lengths of restraining walls needed to be built along with locks, lock keepers' cottages and many other features. The original Newark Town lock and lock keeper's cottage can still be seen at Lock Entry, close to the junction of Castle Gate and Mill Gate.

The effect of this canalisation was to facilitate the two-way transport of goods, from the Humber all the way to Shardlow, a few miles upstream of Nottingham, where the Trent and Mersey Canal, opened in 1760, joined the Trent, thus providing a water link between Newark and the west coast. With much improved roads serving the town and improved river facilities, the stage was set for Newark to enjoy a new prosperity – almost!

Better access from the north via Muskham Road resulted in more traffic feeding into a narrow bridge with a wooden deck and furthermore, although there was enough water now to allow barges to go to Nottingham and beyond and back, the stone piers of the bridge were too close to permit passage of larger boats, partly defeating the object of providing deeper water.

In 1775, the Duke of Newcastle had a bridge designed and built with wider and higher arches. This bridge is on the same site as that built by Bishop Alexander in the 12th century, and is still in use, although footways were added in 1848.

The necessary collection of tolls required the construction of a new tollhouse, also still extant. In parts it is substantially rebuilt and now serves as headquarters for the Nottinghamshire Area Women's Institute.

Although it is considered by some that the malting and brewing industry was not part of the industrial revolution but merely the tail end of the agrarian revolution, it had already become commercialised and increasingly mechanised, with larger concerns already established well before 1775. There are strong arguments to support the notion that the industrial age had already begun albeit with agricultural bias. Malting too was creating employment for a number of people, possibly some of the builders who were unable to work in winter. Malting, unlike today when it is a year round activity, was mainly restricted to the period October to April, the other months being too warm.

CODDINGTON RACES

On occasions even the minute books of Corporations can make interesting reading. An account of horse races to be held on Coddington Moor under the direction of Newark Corporation is one of them.

Although an agreement laying down all conditions to be observed at Coddington horse races (in a later era called more correctly Newark races at Coddington) was not made until March 1st 1624, the minutes of the Newark Corporation include details of the event from 1619. There may even have been races prior to that date, which further scrutiny of the records may reveal, but an interval of five years would seem adequate enough, even for a ponderous corporation, to fulfil the needs for the drawing up regulations.

It was decreed that races were to be held on May 4th each year. Whit Monday, a moveable occasion in those days, seems to have been the day used each year and was probably the implicit intention in 1624.

All competitors had to weigh ten stones – with weights added to achieve this weight. No discussion or condition is laid down for anyone over this weight. Whether such persons were allowed to race with this handicap or were excluded is a question that must remain unanswered. A twenty-shilling piece was the entrance fee, all riders to be assembled between nine and ten o'clock at the start on Coddington Moor, the mounts already saddled and fully shod and carrying the cor-

rect weight. Horseboxes, of course, were unavailable so it can only be conjectured that the participating horses had already been ridden to the site.

Every horse and rider had to complete each of three heats, each of four miles. Half an hour was to be allowed between heats in which to rub down the horse and give it a drink of wholesome water, but no other refreshment was allowed.

At the end of each heat, each horse more than 240 yards behind the winner had to be withdrawn. Of the remaining competitors, the hindmost had to pay the winner of the heat one twenty-shilling piece, always providing there were more than two riders remaining. Should any horse or rider fall, the other competitors must stop and wait until the fallen rider had his foot back in the stirrup. Such behaviour, although gentlemanly, would have been much less appreciated by the horse.

It was stated that no 'man or boy who was either a party to the horse, or who had placed a bet on one, was allowed to strike or otherwise spur it on'. It would thus appear that the fairer sex were not expected to attend – maybe even expressly excluded – although no such instruction is made in the agreement.

After all three heats, the overall winner was weighed again to ensure that his weight was still ten stones, just one pound loss being allowed as wastage, by sweating presumably. He would in due course receive the silver gilt cup (which he kept) plus all the entrance fees, barring the one twenty-shilling piece. The second rider would have his entrance fee reimbursed. A free go! Now there's generous. Such generosity was extended to freemen of the Borough of Newark upon Trent. They were privileged to participate without charge.

Prizes were not awarded immediately after the event. Despite the fact that the Alderman of Newark together with his Serjantes at Mace had to bring the trophy and display it at the meet, he and his escorts were to take it back to Newark, where it was presented to the winner, along with the collected stake money, whereupon he, the winner, was then required to pay the Alderman ten shillings for the hire of the scales and weights and the painting of the course marker posts. Furthermore, in 1624, when the agreement of rules was drawn up, the winner also had to pay five shillings for the engrossing of it. Apparently, even then, there was no such thing as a free ride where local government is involved.

There is no direct specification of where this presentation was to take place, although vague mentions of meeting at The Hart occasionally occur, so maybe a few samples of the local brew were imbibed; purely for medicinal purposes, of course.

The first silver double gilt cup was purchased in 1619 weighing 23 ½ ounces, at a cost of seven shillings an ounce, making the total paid £8 - 4s. It was specified that the cup should always weigh about 22 ounces. Donations from *'divers Noblemen and Gentlemen in the Countie of Nottingham'* were gathered to finance the setting up of the tradition. The Newark Coat of Arms was to be engraved upon the cup at a cost of 5 shillings and additionally a flying horse was to be provided costing 3s - 4d to be procured, along with a box to put the cup in adding a further 4 pence. The silversmith was not reimbursed until the time of the following event. This annual event continued until interrupted by the English Civil War in 1642.

A representative of a local auction house has never seen, nor even heard of a Newark Cup being offered for sale and from this it can only be concluded that most were donated to the town when besieged in the Civil War to facilitate the striking of Newark siege coins, examples of which can still be seen in various local repositories.

It is believed that the races did not resume until the 19th century when there was a newspaper advertisement for Newark Races for Friday 3rd September 1841 at twelve o'clock with no less than five races, each to be run in two or three heats, each with a very worthwhile prize, the highest of which, The Tradesman's Purse was worth twelve sovereigns plus a sweepstake; of all the sovereign stakes barring that of the runner up, who kept his stake as reward. The Farmers' Plate, ten sovereigns plus sweepstake, the Ladies Purse only seven. Each male winner paid two pounds towards expenses, and the lady one pound.

Although the social hierarchy is still in evidence here, ladies are now admitted, encouraged even, in contrast to the previous era. Horses were entered at the Robin Hood Hotel the previous evening and the start was not until eleven o'clock. Newark Races at Coddington continued until 1877 when noncompliance with Jockey Club rules brought it to an end. A descendant of one of the contestants reports that races using donkeys were held for a few years, but were soon discontinued.

A Short History of Newark by Hodgkinson provides further interesting reading on Coddington Races.

NEWARK LIVESTOCK MARKET

An idyllic view of cows or sheep peacefully grazing in a meadow is a quintessential image of country life in Britain. However without the very necessary hedges, fences and grass kept short by continual grazing by livestock, the patchwork quilt of changing arable crops would be very different. Without the rural economy England would be a much poorer country in sense of both landscape and wealth.

The self-descriptive Newark Livestock Market focuses attention on the much more serious aspects of farming life. The very reason for its existence was and is to generate income; in times past often only at subsistence level, but today providing some disposable income too.

Most fascinating to watch is the assorted assembly of people gathered there on market day, such as the farmers, many with the ubiquitous cloth cap worn awry and ready to be lifted using finger and thumb, which enables the scratching of the top of the head with the three free fingers – a distinct aid to concentration.

Until the very ornate Ossington Coffee Palace was built at the junction of the Great North Road and Castlegate in 1883, not only did the cattle market occupy part of the site upon which that fine building stands, but it spread across the full width of the road to encroach upon what is now part of the Castle gardens, as far as the Gilstrap Centre wall. A sign on the wall confirms that the site is still called Beast Market Hill.

Once the coffee house and Gilstrap Library were built in 1883, conditions in the cattle market rendered it somewhat unsavoury for the patrons of both establishment. Land was bought on the other side of Trent Bridge on the corner of Tolney Lane, and in 1885 the pigs, sheep and cattle market moved to the new site where it was to remain for over 80 years, before moving to its present site near the relief road.

Remaining in the middle of the road on the old site, where the Castle roundabout now is, was the rabbits, poultry and general effects auction. The auctioneer occupied a small portable shed from which goods were sold. The first Christmas, free of the encumbrances now removed across the river, sales of poultry, geese in particular, were very brisk; a very profitable auction indeed. Cyril Hopewell, the auctioneer, was heard to remark that it was 'a bit draughty'. The headline in the *Newark Advertiser* the following week read, *'Auctioneer Feels The Draught'*, where upon the auction was moved to the wharf where it remained until just before the millennium.

Although now moved across the river, ask any Newark-born visitor to the auction market where the purchase of the lawnmower or other artefact was made and still they will answer, "On the 'ill!" Now that's tradition!

The importance of the general effects auction, where one man's junk becomes another's income is very much in evidence. Poorer echelons do frequent the market, but many of the regulars make quite a reasonable living, replenishing their stock of all manner of items to sell at car boot sales in the locale.

MALTING AND BREWING

Before mains water supplies became available, many sources of water were unsafe to drink. Boiling the water for ten minutes kills off many pathogens. The fermentation process was discovered accidentally by the Egyptians 6000 years ago, when dried bread became wet. The combined effect of boiling together with the antiseptic properties of alcohol rendered the water from the fermentation almost completely safe to drink, and with a taste not too unpleasant and easily acquired, and with a strange ameliorating effect, it soon gained favour.

It wasn't long before it was discovered that it was not necessary to bake bread as a basic ingredient. This mysterious liquid could be obtained by pouring boiling water directly onto the grain especially if it had dried in the sun. Beer was born.

Experiments, galore probably, gradually refined the process until beer of great strength could be obtained when compared with today's alcoholic content. This continuous testing and tasting still continues today. Why wouldn't it? If it ain't broke, why fix it? It is a well-known fact that there is no such drink as bad beer; some just taste much better than others. The incidence of water-borne infections reduced dramatically.

Barley was discovered to be the best grain with which to make beer but scientific reasons were not actually discovered until comparatively recent times. The process of growing the barley by soaking it and then spreading it on the floor to grow turns the starches in the grain into sugars, maltose if you must know. It is these sugars, extracted from the grain with boiling water, cooled and then yeast added that causes the fermentation. Barley from poorer, sandy loams, is much thinner skinned and therefore is more readily affected, hence more suited for this treatment.

Most manor houses, estate farmhouses and vicarages had a brew house and mostly a malt house too. Everyone in the household drank beer, the strongest being reserved for the top table. It had long been discovered that having made one batch of beer, a second and sometimes even a third brew could be obtained. Each subsequent brew was less potent than the previous. The third brew known as small beer, was reserved for children and those who were easily intoxicated, hence the use of the expression 'small beer' to denote someone of less than adequate capabilities, or children.

Malt kilns, where the grown grain was dried, are easily recognised with their square plan and pagoda roof, and many still retain the characteristic window openings, albeit now bricked in. Many others have been converted and may be a little harder to spot. There are two examples in Morton, one at Manor Farm and the other next to the church. There is an excellent example of a small malt house cum brew house to the rear of The White Swan in Newark. Although it is now converted to a toilet block, the characteristic outline of the windows can still be discerned.

In some instances, malting, brewing and baking were all effected in the same building, thus making maximum, virtually continuous use of the building, the same furnace being used for boiling water or baking by clever use of different flues. There is a candidate for this category in Southwell, although documentary evidence proves elusive.

Malthouses are often very easy to identify, but paradoxically, recognition can be virtually impossible where conversion to accommodation has occurred. The malthouse in East Markham is intact and unaltered, although now used for crop storage. Standing along side what was the main road until the road was straightened and re-sited twenty yards away, identification is simplicity itself. Even the vents with the characteristic sliding shutters are still present. Unfortunately, the double kiln with its furnaces, which were situated behind the malthouses, has been demolished.

By contrast, in Farnsfield, the shell and much of the interior structure of a whole malting complex is still extant, although the kiln block is much altered and would be unrecognisable, were it not in context. The whole structure has been skillfully modified to form a useful village community centre. Most villagers were, until informed, blissfully unaware of its former purpose.

At Carlton-on-Trent there were three which were larger, all belonging to Samuel Hole of Caunton who malted his own barley before selling it to breweries. There may be others in Carlton, but they remain unidentified. These kilns were built alongside corresponding couching houses, where the grain was soaked and grown.

Southwell has been fortunate too. Of the three malthouses mentioned in records, two remain, but converted; of the third only one wall, up to chest height, survives. Malting was never going to achieve great status here. Mostly, the town is surrounded by heavy clay land, ideal for hops and wheat, but not well suited to the production of malting grade barley, hence the predominance of flour milling in the town.

Opposite the Bromley Arms in Fiskerton are the converted remains of malt kilns. These are relics of a later era than the above although older maltings were to be found here too. Those still on the wharf also at one time belonged to Samuel Hole. Being a commercial maltster, he favoured riverside locations since these gave him easy transport of both barley from the lighter lands of the Trent Valley and finished malt to various brewers, his son James Hole who was also a maltster, amongst them.

Two enormous concrete maltings alongside the Trent close by the bridge in Newark, apart from their distinction as the first commercial use of poured concrete, and listed monuments as a result, were built for Lord Manners-Sutton of Kelham, but bought by Samuel Hole and worked by son James, who changed to brewing when malt tax was repealed in 1880. Shortly afterwards he bought the brewery of Caparn and Hankey in Albert Street, Newark, significantly called Castle Brewery, where he prospered to become one of the two largest brewers in the town. There were as many as ten smaller breweries in Newark, most of which were periodically absorbed by the firm Warwick and Richardson, which became the other large brewery in Newark.

Speculative building of a large malting and brewing complex by Newark Town Wharf in 1766 marked the launch of large-scale commercial enterprises in Newark. Samuel Sketchley junior who learned his trade with his father, a successful brewer in Burton-on-Trent, was engaged to run the business. That he made a success of it can be judged by the fact that he became Mayor several times and owned property in Newark in his own right. On the death of Sketchley, the complex was bought by Richard Warwick, the first of his acquisitions.

When Trent Brewery in Millgate, Newark, owned by Richardson, Earp and Slater, had expanded to full capacity, Slater died and, needing to realise their assets, the other partners elected to sell up. It was bought by Richard Warwick, who was by now, very successful. He was joined by Joseph Richardson in Northgate as a partner to become Warwick and Richardson, Brewers. Thomas Earp joined William Gilstrap, formerly an hotelier before the coming of the railways made that trade less profitable and he turned to malting, to form Gilstrap, Earp and Company, which was to become the largest producer of malt in the town. Both companies prospered and expanded.

Another maltster, Henry Branston was also very progressive, becoming Mayor in his turn. The families of these various businessmen became, over the course of time, related by marriage. The Gilstraps and Branstons were already so connected, but a hat-trick of marriages of three Branston girls to three Warwick brothers cemented an already convoluted family hierarchy. Most of the malting families had such ties, some closer than others. To itemise it would require a book of its own, but nevertheless it could be demonstrated that it was the cross fertilisation of successful business families that was to turn Newark into the Metropolis of Malt.

Antiquated plant on valuable development sites and the introduction of much more productive methods of producing malt all year round, rather than just during the cooler months and being concentrated by modern docks in Ipswich, have taken the toll of malting in the whole country. The Clean Rivers Act drove in the final coffin nail in the mid-fifties.

Both Holes Brewery and Warwick and Richardson were themselves taken over by John Smith and Courage respectively in 1966. The smells of drying malt and brewer's grains no longer fill the air of Newark, odours that are fondly remembered by many older residents.

Many of the redundant malthouses have, over the years, fallen victim to fire – both accidental and otherwise – demolition and decay. Some of the survivors have been adapted for business use, many converted to apartments and a few wrecks await their fate.

The heavier clay land was ideally suited to hops. On examination of Sanderson's map – twenty miles round Mansfield – indicates many sites where hops were grown. Mine host at the Hop Pole Inn at Ollerton grew hops very profitably, malted barley and brewed beer all successfully, as well as maintaining the inn. When the advent of railways crippled the coaching inn trade, it is possible that his ancillary occupations were sufficient to augment the money from his much reduced hotel trade. The Hop Pole still looks inviting and profitable, but maltings in the yard stand derelict and redundant.

TURNPIKES IN THE DISTRICT

Regulations existed from Tudor times that required each individual parish to maintain its own roads. Mostly of course, these roads served rural communities and really were adequate only for local users, farmers and tradesmen for instance, but for long distance travellers they were far from satisfactory.

As trade increased in the late 17th century, the increasing number of heavy carts, wagons and carriages resulted in serious damage to major routes, repairs for which the previous provision of statute labour was unable to provide. Parliamentary Acts were introduced at this time, piecemeal at first, empowering local justices to ensure the adequate maintenance of a section of the highway. This system too proved most unsatisfactory, only affecting isolated sections rather that a more

beneficial whole.

Early in the 18th century, Turnpike Acts were introduced allowing trusts to administer funds provided by the several parishes through which the road passed, to ensure and pay for maintenance on that section. Trustees were selected from local gentry, merchants and clergy who paid officials to administer the schemes. Better transport meant easier access to markets and increased trade and consequently higher rents, all to the benefit of the trustees.

Less fortunate were the inhabitants of villages not on these turnpike roads, which also derived income from tolls collected at the start of each section. Many of these villages found themselves required to maintain these major roads which they never used, but had no time to maintain the rural roads upon which they depended. Many such roads disappeared altogether whilst others continued, and still do, as farm tracks or bridleways, the latter often reduced to access for hikers but serving no other economic purpose at all.

Occasionally, the isolation so caused led to the complete decline of a village. Barnby-in-the-Willows, at the eastern extremity of the district, was on the main coach road from Newark to Sleaford, until the Turnpike Act for the Leadenham to Farnsfield stretch of what is now the A17, bypassed it altogether. The original road from Newark to Barnby still exists, but only as far as the village, the footbridge across the appropriately named Shire Dyke now offering onto a mere footpath on the Lincolnshire side, and eventually peters out altogether. The village, at the end of a cul de sac, has become a dormitory for Newark businessmen, teachers and retirees. The Willow Tree, being a small coaching inn, was reduced to the status of a village pub, with repercussions both for staff and suppliers.

Hazelford, the very name redolent of an earlier era, and the ferry that served it, was on the main carriage route from Newark to Nottingham, before turnpiking of the Fosse rendered the route obsolescent, the route using the Fosse and the Grantham road, giving the advantages of a better road surface and obviating the need for and inconvenience of a ferry crossing; an even greater advantage when the Trent was in spate. The former inn is now a retirement home.

There are other villages within the district with similar tales to tell. As in many things in life, there are winners and losers. Numerous once-isolated hamlets prospered because the route of the turnpike road passed their way.

Newark, Southwell, Tuxford and Ollerton were all market towns; the first three still are, Ollerton, alas, is not. All were almost exclusively reliant upon agriculture either directly as exchanges of goods, often by barter, or indirectly as a regular meeting place where travelling tradesmen provide good or services not always available in smaller villages and hamlets. Significantly all were at the junctions of major highways, a factor that was to stand them in good stead when these roads were turnpiked.

Newark, sited on the Great North Road, which at that time actually passed through the very centre of the town via Baldertongate and Dry Bridge, now Bridge Street, into the market square, where access could be gained to the numerous inns of the town. This route was joined at Dry Bridge by Barnbygate, such appellation serving as a reminder of the importance at that time of Barnby in the Willows, the very suffix being necessary to avoid confusion with Barnby in the Moor, just a few miles further north.

The Fosse brought in travellers from Lincoln and Nottingham; the Great North Road from Grantham and Retford, passing through Tuxford en route and the Ollerton Road from Mansfield via Farnsfield and Southwell facilitated passage. There are sufficient examples here to illustrate the sheer volume of traffic that was already on the roads, each passenger needing varying degrees of service on arrival such as a comfort stop, food and drink or overnight accommodation.

Many also came to do business in the town. Similar facilities were, of course, required at any such town, Newark is just an example.

The advent of turnpiking was a blessing for travellers. Journey times were cut by as much as a third, but an additional bonus accruing from the easier going meant that the horses were able to cover greater distances. A journey of twelve to fourteen miles was now possible without changing horses. Although the faster times had a negative effect on the profitability of coaching inns, this circumstance was more than amply compensated by the much greater number of travellers. It was boom time for the inns.

On balance, this significant increase in income for the innkeepers was reflected in the income of any such town, as increased trade supplying the needs, or in local employment. To be a victualler was to become very rich indeed, even where financial irregularities did not occur.

Just as canal mania and turnpiking were making fortunes for some, along came the railway age. Initially, innkeepers were unconcerned, thinking that although passengers would arrive by train, changes to coach travel would be necessary to complete the journey. To some extent this was true, but not for long. Although as railway mania thrived, rail connections to many obscure villages were constructed; and so they remained until Dr Beeching, the transport minister, 'rationalised' the railways, resulting in many branch lines being closed.

Trade at the inns plummeted. Not realised by most people was that because journey times were so reduced, business men travelling from say London to York, could do both outward and return journeys and conduct their business all in one day, all with a greater degree of comfort, even in open-top carriages. There were no potholes. Trains ran to a schedule. The days of unexpected delays were virtually over.

William Gilstrap reacted to the turndown in trade by introducing a horse and trap taxi service to and from the two stations, but people with business to conduct formed the greater part of these. As elsewhere, they were ready to return whence they came within less than a day. Gone was the virtually insatiable need for hotel accommodation. William Gilstrap sold his hotel in Kirkgate well before the final demise of the trade, transferring his assets into the burgeoning malting industry. As there was a malthouse with the hotel, he did have experience of the trade. A neighbouring businessman bought or rented these malthouses, which were actually in his back yard. Recently qualified as a grocer, he had set up his grocery and seed merchants shop. The opportunity to add another string was too good to miss. Those readers possessed of a crystal ball may have realised that this young entrepreneur was Henry Branston who was to found the Branston malting dynasty, met earlier.

Records seem to show that many people in Ollerton had two employments, sometimes seasonally complementary, or sometimes as a full and a part time job. By this means, maybe, they were able to earn sufficient money from their other activities when the inn trade was lost.

History is repeating itself, as oft it does. Newark, Tuxford and Retford are now bypassed by the A1, the dual-carriageway supercession to the turnpike. Whereas the railways at least pass through the town and often stop there, to travellers on the A1, covering in an hour or so a distance needing at least a twelve hour day before, the names of the towns – are just that – a name only, barely noticed or remembered. That's progress!

THE EAKRING OIL FIELD

Whilst walking in Duke's Wood at Eakring amongst the wild flowers and the trees listening to the numerous species of birds and catching the occasional glimpse of a small land-based mammal scurrying for cover as its peace and solitude is disturbed, it is hard to imagine the frenetic activity here of 1943.

German U-boats were wreaking havoc on merchant shipping, particularly oil tankers. An Admiralty report stated that reserves of oil, normally five million barrels, were down to three. In addition to the lost tankers, nearly one million barrels were lost in bombing raids on the docks. Enough oil for just two months was available. An emergency meeting of the Oil Control Board was called. Even the possibility of a negotiated settlement with Germany was considered.

At this meeting a representative of D'Arcy Oil Exploration revealed a secret – large quantities of oil located beneath Sherwood Forest, Duke's Wood specifically. The problem was getting it out of the ground quickly enough to avert disaster.

American rednecks, naturally very well skilled in the art of drilling, were recruited and quickly helped to drill the extra 106 wells needed. Much of the necessary equipment also came from America. By the end of the war, the combined output of Eakring and Dukes Wood was about three million gallons from 240 wells. This oil, having a low sulphur content, was of superior quality and after refinement it was ideally suited to the Rolls Royce engines fitted to many of our aircraft.

Eakring oil field was one of the best-kept secrets of the war until a national newspaper ran an 'exclusive' report. Was it a treasonable offence, or was the information carefully leaked in order to boost the nation's morale? The Secretary for Petroleum at the time, Geoffrey Lloyd, on a press visit to Dukes Wood commented:

'This oilfield like Britain, is small but of the highest quality, it yields a whole range of refinery petroleum products. Milk and oil from the same field is the slogan here. This oilfield came into operation just when we needed every ton of oil to carry this country through the crisis of the war. These were supplies that the U-boats could never sink.'*

* Cited in Dukes Wood Oil Museum website.

The rednecks were billeted at Kelham Hall, alongside monks of the Society for the Sacred Mission. Because their tasks were arduous, and the working day long, the rednecks were allowed extra rations. In their free time they repaired to the nearby Kelham Fox to savour a pint or two, although, perhaps, savour is hardly the right word. Never did they come to really like the warm, bitter beer. Perhaps the temperature of the beer was tolerable, but they put salt in the beer to take away the bitterness much to the amusement of the locals. What their reaction was to Brussels sprouts is not recorded.

Duke's Wood is now a Site of Special Scientific Interest. The various effluents, waste by-products of the oil extraction process, prove to provide an ideal environment for rare orchids and other flowers to flourish. Within the wood is a heritage museum with many photographs and items of memorabilia where the whole story can be explored and a 'nodding donkey' observed up close, the well below long since exhausted. There are still a small number of active pumps around the area.

THE BRAMLEY APPLE OF SOUTHWELL

A blue plaque on the wall of a house in Easthorpe Southwell locates the garden in which the original Bramley apple tree still grows. Famous throughout the land for its looks and culinary perfection, having won numerous awards, the Bramley apple is celebrated in the town having given its name to a pub and a local newspaper, not to mention the annual Bramley competition, where numerous pies, baked to treasured recipes, vie one against the other for the first prize.

The history of the discovery and development of this variety begins with the birth of Henry Merryweather, in Carlton-on-Trent in 1839. His father, also Henry, described his son as having the makings of a fine nurseryman being, as he was, very observant and knowledgeable regarding the cultivation of all types of fruit trees.

Whilst about his business, the seventeen-year-old Henry,

came upon the gardener for the Vicar Choral at the Minster, carrying a basket of fine apples. Henry learned that these were old Mr Bramley's apples. Not recognising the variety Henry immediately went to see Mr Bramley and his tree, which at the time was laden with beautiful fruit.

*"I was struck by the marvellous appearance of this wonderful fruit and Mr Bramley said 'It is my apple and raised in my garden and is called Bramley's Seedling'."**

Henry enquired if he might have some grafts and was told to take what he wanted.

*"From that time I worked all the plants I had room for and by degrees had a fine stock of young plants."**

The first recorded sale in Henry Merryweather's accounts was on 31st October 1862: *'3 Bramley's for 2/- to Mr George Cooper of Upton Hall'*. (Just a fraction over 3p each in modern terms). By 1885 it was known as the 'King of all apples'. In the Merryweather catalogue for 1896/7 it states that *'Mr Merryweather has 350,000 fruit trees to select from'* – although not all Bramleys of course.

Garden Illustrated of 1924 states that *'if you only plant one tree, let it be a Bramley. One tree will pay the rent of a cottage.'*

In 1944, the original tree blew down, leaving some five feet of trunk in contact with the ground, which rooted at the first limb. Judicious pruning has ensured that the tree still prospers.

* From his diary cited in *The Bramley Apple Story* by Roger Merryweather.

THE OLDE WHITE HART, NEWARK

Hidden behind the 15th century arch are parts of the original coaching inn, dating to 1313. To the right was the hall to the complex which has been archaeologically explored and the timber dated. Now converted to boutiques, a step or two back allows observation of the fascinating twisted roof as the timbers have shrunk and contorted over the years. These contortions are commonplace with timber-framed houses but in this one are particularly pronounced. Looking back towards Market Place, to the right of the arch stands a renovated turret staircase granting access to the gallery which is best seen from the market square.

Substantially renovated in the 1960s the front range, facing the historic cobbled square, dates from the 15th century and boasts a crown post roof. The highly decorated upper storeys have been faithfully recreated using existing remnants as patterns.

The earthy red decoration is a welcome change from the much more common Victorian affectation of black and white. Timber-framed houses would not have been painted in sharply contrasting colours – occasionally the wood might have been lime washed. The colours here are believed to be reasonably authentic.

Just above the ground floor windows and arch are twenty-four effigies, some representing St. Barbara and the other St. Anthony of Padua. A few of those at the left end are originals, the remainder are stone casts, supposedly 12 of each but actually the are 11 of one and 13 of the other.

There is an amusing story regarding the pierced fretwork ornamentation of the upper storey windows. Because the style of fretwork used in the rood screen of the Parish Church of St. Mary Magdalene bears a reasonable resemblance to that seen here, the traditional tale is that the carpenters working in the church were unable to settle the bill at the Olde White Hart. The landlord of the inn, never one to miss the chance of a profit, allegedly suggested that they carve the ornamentation for his façade, a reasonable enough story but without any documentary corroboration whatever.

When it was built, the White Hart, as it then was, stood very close to the Great North Road which at that time passed along Baldertongate and then Bridge Street which is just a few yards away, across Market Place and out via Kirkgate to reach the Trent Bridge on its way northward, or, of course, vice versa. The symbol of a White Hart was a timely reference to Richard II. A white hart formed part of his coat of arms.

THE CONCRETE BARGE

Close by the Trent in Holme parish lies Winthorpe Lake. Why the place celebrates the adjacent village is a mystery. Created by the Hull Sand and Gravel Company in the years just prior to World War II, with a short navigable channel connecting it to the river, it is, in plainer terms, a redundant gravel pit, grandly titled Winthorpe Lake.

Before the days of landscaping such places, when they fell into disuse they occasionally became graveyards for scrap barges. This is one such. Rusting hulls line one edge, each with a fascinating history to recount, but little opportunity to tell it. Lying now, three parts buried by the sands of time, these once proud vessels gradually disappear into oblivion, just like the busy industrial period of prosperity for the district that they and their masters helped to create. One such relic, much larger than the rest, is not steel but concrete and still able to arouse some interest, though usually nothing more than idle curiosity, nevertheless giving birth to several plausible but erroneous conjectures, and other more fanciful and equally wrong uses attributed.

Built experimentally, when steel was expensive and cheaper alternatives were sought, such craft were never destined to be commercial successes. With a steel skeleton and wearing a moulded concrete jacket, these broad-in-the-beam barges were, as a consequence, very heavy, the latter property demanding deeper water and the former necessitating wide-arched bridges. Neither condition is commonplace even on rivers of more ample proportion.

A collection of such barges was used for emergency storage of cargo, normally held in warehouses at the Humber ports, as with German bombing raids causing grievous damage, safe dispersal of vital goods to these lighters gave them an absolutely vital, if very brief, moment of glory.

Passage through Trent Bridge in Newark proved impossible and such circumstances denied this relic the more glorious use as an attraction at a new marina. Winthorpe Lake was used as a berth whilst an alternative was found. Here fate took a hand. In gale force winds one night the craft, at anchor in the deep mid-lake water, broke free, being driven before the wind onto the bank, assuming a rakish angle as it did so. First thoughts were to refloat it, but the process would have been difficult and with no other practical uses in mind, a decision

to abandon it was taken, with the hull holed to prevent any impromptu refloating. And so it remains, albeit not in the first flush of youth, with much of the timber decking now rotted away and trees growing in the hold, finding sufficient anchorage and nourishment in the deposited silt, a unique element of the landscape of Holme.

Saxon Bridge at Cromwell

The *Nottingham Daily Guardian* for February 20th 1877 reported that an elderly employee of the Trent Navigation Company, many years previously had,

'helped clear away a lozenge-shaped bridge pier formed of trees laid on the bed of the river and the enclosed space filled with Coddington stone, at a site 2-300 yards downstream of the 'oven', an island south of Cromwell.'

Work commenced in 1884 to remove two further piers, which had obstructed routine dredging near Cromwell. Until the construction of a lock here, the Trent was tidal almost as far as Newark, resulting in laden boats grounding at low water.

This essential dredging work was obstructed by what turned out to be two further piers. Compton, an archaeologist in a subsequent report wrote, *'In three hours eight charges of dy-*

namite judiciously disposed, completely wrecked the remains of work which had withstood the activities of weather and water for sixteen centuries.'

Luckily detailed dimensions of the piers were recorded, and photographs were taken before the demolition, along with details of the construction. Timbers, the only ones known to have survived, were rescued and are now preserved in the Newark Museum Resource Centre. Erroneous interpretation of a carpenter's mark had dated the bridge as 2nd century Roman, but recent analysis by dendrochronology places felling of the timber shortly before the middle of the 8th century, a date which has been confirmed by radio carbon dating, some six centuries later than had been supposed in 1884.

Standing beside the lock at Cromwell is a 'memorial' stone recording the date of the removal of piers in 1884. That it was such an unceremonious removal is not remarked upon. Construction of a lock at Cromwell determined the new boundary of the tidal Trent.

Wellow and the Maypole

From time immemorial, a day of celebration centred on the tradition of dancing around the Maypole at Wellow, culminating in the crowning of the new May Queen and the retirement of her predecessor. In recent times, only during the two World Wars have festivities been interrupted, amongst other things because rehearsal space became emergency accommodation for the military.

Traditionally held on Whit Monday, now spring Bank Holiday it is reassuring to witness the continuation of the event which necessitates the closure of Eakring Road; just one day in the year when the car is not king. In clement weather, the event draws an attendance of about 2500, most of whom arrive early in order to enjoy the other entertainments by the sides of the village green and in the Red Lion car park wherein cars are banished for the day.

Instead here can be found a temporary bar arranged under a canopy to ease the pressure inside the quaint and intimate timber-framed pub itself. Nearer the street at various times, a street entertainer performs juggling skills with audience participation both physically and orally, just like a pantomime. By way of a change, and a well-earned rest for him, Morrismen perform several traditional dances, giving way to sword dancers, or to a group of wandering minstrels.

A display of birds of prey on the wide grass verge attracts quite a crowd; some of the birds – a peregrine falcon in particular – revelling in the glory, posing any time cameras are raised. Almost unnoticed, perched on the boundary rope, a cock robin, obviously alarmed by the presence of this predator, demonstrates his courage by threatening the falcon, who seems to remain oblivious to the threat.

The tiniest toddlers still shriek with delight at Rat-Up-a-Drainpipe as they have since longer ago than anyone can remember. A great grandfather of some vintage recalls when he played the game as a child.

Maypole dancing, first by the smallest children, some maybe as young as five, then followed in years of seniority, is a main attraction. Each year performs a dance whereby the ribbons are braided in different patterns, each successive dance more complicated than the previous one.

Judging by the number of early teenagers pelting wet sponges with great gusto at the 'willing' victim, it could well be a teacher with his head in the hole. Harmless enough in itself, but it recall the more serious pillory punishment of yesteryear.

Wellow has the distinction of being the only moated village in England. Apparently this was dug to prevent attack and pillaging by neighbouring villages. It is difficult to imagine any of the villages nearby being so unruly; everywhere seems to exude peace and serenity. It was not always so, apparently.

A Tale of Two Bridges

François Hennebique is not a name that rolls off the tongues of many residents of the district and yet many avail themselves of the services provided by his invention. Anglers, dog-walkers and other pedestrians make fairly regular use of what is colloquially called Elbow Bridge, although known to the Institute of Civil Engineers, and probably more correctly, as Fiddler's Elbow Bridge.

The Hennebique system was one of the first reinforced concrete methods of construction, and the bridge, erected in 1915 by Leonard Mouchel, uses a unique system of cross connected bars of iron as a base for the batch-mixed concrete. Only six inches thick at the crest, this semi-circular arch is an elegant example of this early industrial use of concrete in Newark, and one reason for it being a listed monument. It is considered by many industrial archaeologists that wrought iron was used in the construction of this bridge – such material not being susceptible to rust. Certainly, as recent examinations have revealed, there is no sign of concrete sickness here: surely a testament to the effectiveness of both the design and durability of materials.

Constructed as a roving bridge, a feature found often on narrow canals where the towpath changed sides, and by means of an underpass beneath the bridge, the horse passed through and then over the bridge. This manoeuvre could be effected without unhitching the horse. Employment of the technique for the much wider river is virtually unique, necessitating as it does a very long hauling rope. That said, the greater length meant a straighter, more efficient pull. Rope burns on the abutment show that the bridge was so used.

In 1922, when it was deemed necessary to replace the bridge at Muskham, Hennebique's system was again employed, this time though, using stainless steel as the ribs. Muskham Bridge, built to carry vehicular traffic, is supported by piers. This road carries the Great North Road over the Kelham branch of the Trent and until 1962 when the A1 Newark bypass was opened, carried the full volume of A1 traffic.

Even today, a steady stream of traffic crosses the river by this means, a stream joined on numerous occasions, when traffic accidents block the A1 and necessitates diversion through the town, endorsing once again the success of the Hennebique system, which regrettably, has in its turn been superseded by inventions and use of pre-stressed concrete beams for bridge support – equally effective and cheaper too perhaps, but no-where near as elegant!

Just as the junction of important highways led to the formation of Newark, the gradual improvement of these routes has resulted in increasing trade and prosperity for the town.

On Friday June 27th 2009, the first sod was cut, signalling the commencement of conversion to dual carriageway of the Fosse. This long awaited road improvement heralds a new phase in Newark's history. Much relief from congestion will be enjoyed by travellers on the road and a new peace and calm will descend upon the few villages that will be by-passed.

Visible from the new road will be the new Staythorpe power station, already half built, from which power carrying pylons stride across the Trent Valley into the future – Newark and Sherwood's future.

This title is one in a new series by **Cottage Publications**.
For more information and to see our other titles, please visit our website
www.cottage-publications.com
or alternatively you can contact us as follows:–

Telephone: +44 (0)28 9188 8033
Fax: +44 (0)28 9188 8063

Cottage Publications
is an imprint of
Laurel Cottage Ltd.,
15 Ballyhay Road,
Donaghadee, Co. Down,
N. Ireland, BT21 0NG